Plural Maghreb

Suspensions: Contemporary Middle Eastern and Islamicate Thought

Series editors: Jason Bahbak Mohaghegh and Lucian Stone
This series interrupts standardized discourses involving the Middle East and the Islamicate world by introducing creative and emerging ideas. The incisive works included in this series provide a counterpoint to the reigning canons of theory, theology, philosophy, literature, and criticism through investigations of vast experiential typologies—such as violence, mourning, vulnerability, tension, and humour—in light of contemporary Middle Eastern and Islamicate thought.

Other titles in this series include:

Plural Maghreb

Writings on Postcolonialism

Abdelkebir Khatibi

Translated by
P. Burcu Yalim

BLOOMSBURY ACADEMIC
LONDON • NEW YORK • OXFORD • NEW DELHI • SYDNEY

BLOOMSBURY ACADEMIC
Bloomsbury Publishing Plc
50 Bedford Square, London, WC1B 3DP, UK
1385 Broadway, New York, NY 10018, USA

BLOOMSBURY, BLOOMSBURY ACADEMIC and the Diana logo are trademarks
of Bloomsbury Publishing Plc

First published in France as Maghreb Pluriel by Abdelkebir Khatibi,
Éditions Denoél, 1983

First published in Great Britain 2019

Copyright © Abdelkebir Khatibi and Bloomsbury Publishing Plc, 2019

Lalla Mina El Alaoui Khatibi has asserted Abdelkebir Khatibi's right under the
Copyright, Designs and Patents Act, 1988, to be identified as Author of this work.

For legal purposes, the Acknowledgments on p. viii constitute an extension
of this copyright page.

Cover image: *Kula: Turning Back* (2017), lignire on paper on canvas, 144x144 cm
© Nadia Kaabi-Linke
Photo by Timo Kaabi-Linke, 2017

A catalogue record for this book is available from the British Library.

A catalog record for this book is available from the Library of Congress.

ISBN: HB: 978-1-3500-5394-6
PB: 978-1-3500-5395-3
ePDF: 978-1-3500-5396-0
eBook: 978-1-3500-5397-7

Series: Suspensions: Contemporary Middle Eastern and Islamicate Thought

Typeset by Newgen KnowledgeWorks Pvt. Ltd., Chennai, India
Printed and bound in Great Britain

To find out more about our authors and books, visit www.bloomsbury.com
and sign up for our newsletters.

Contents

Series Foreword

Poets, artists, theologians, philosophers, and mystics in the Middle East and Islamicate world have been interrogating notions of desire, madness, sensuality, solitude, death, time, space, etc. for centuries, thus constituting an expansive and ever-mutating intellectual landscape. Like all theory and creative outpouring, then, theirs is its own vital constellation—a construction cobbled together from singular visceral experiences, intellectual ruins, novel aesthetic techniques, social-political-ideological detours, and premonitions of a future—built and torn down (partially or in toto), and rebuilt again with slight and severe variations. The horizons shift and frequently leave those who dare traverse these lands bewildered and vulnerable.

Consequently, these thinkers and their visionary ideas largely remain unknown, or worse, mispronounced and misrepresented in the so-called Western world. In the hands of imperialistic frameworks, a select few are deemed worthy of notice and are spoken on behalf of, or rather *about*. Their ideas are simplified into mere social formulae and empirical scholarly categories. Whereas so-called Western philosophers and writers are given full leniency to contemplate the most incisive or abstract ideas, non-Western thinkers, especially those located in the imagined realms of the Middle East and Islamicate world, are reduced to speaking of purely political histories or monolithic cultural narratives. In other words, they are distorted and contorted to fit within hegemonic paradigms that steal away their more captivating potentials.

Contributors to this series provide a counterpoint to the reigning canons of theory, theology, philosophy, literature, and criticism through investigations of the vast experiential typologies of such regions. Each volume in the series acts as a "suspension" in the sense that the authors will position contemporary thought in an enigmatic new terrain of inquiry, where it will be compelled to confront unforeseen works of critical and creative imagination. These analyses will not only highlight the full range of current intellectual and artistic trends and their benefits for the citizens of these phantom spheres, but also argue that the ideas themselves are borderless and thus of great relevance to all citizens of the world.

Jason Bahbak Mohaghegh and Lucian Stone

Acknowledgments

Editors' Acknowledgments

The editors of the series would like to express their gratitude to Mme Lalla Mina El Alaoui Khatibi for entrusting them to publish this translation of her late husband's work. Without her support and enthusiasm for this project, it would not have been possible.

We would also like to thank Professor Réda Bensmaïa and Professor Mourad El-Khatibi for their assistance and introducing us to Mme El Alaoui.

Translator's Acknowledgments

I am grateful to Professor Mahmut Mutman who introduced me to Khatibi's thought and in a way made this translation possible. I would also like to thank the series' editors Lucian Stone and Jason Bahbak Mohaghegh again for making this possible, and for their kind assistance and understanding during the whole process.

1

Other-Thought

On decolonization

Shortly before his death, Frantz Fanon made the following call: "Come, then, comrades, the European game has finally ended; we must find something different."[1]

Yes, to find something else, to place oneself according to an other-thought, a thought of difference, perhaps unheard of. Yes, such liberation is rigorously necessary for all thought that thus invokes its will, taking a risk, which in any case can only be great.

But what is the European game in question here? Or rather, must we not *first* postulate that this Europe is still a question that shakes us to the core of our being? This observation marks an interrogation, in other words, an inevitable event, which is neither a disaster nor a blessing, but the condition of a responsibility that remains to be taken, beyond resentment and unhappy consciousness.

This beyond is not a gift of the simple will to revolt. It is a working on the self, a constant work to transform one's suffering, humiliation, and depression in the relationship with the other and others. Focusing on such questions marks a grief, and I would say, a grief without hope or despair, without finality in itself, but altogether a global necessity that life imposes on us only to abandon us to the same question, the first and the last: that there is no choice.

Let us clarify. In any event, the core of our being, touched and tormented by the so-called Western will to power, this innermost element that suffers from humiliation and violent and stupefying domination, cannot be resolved by a naïve declaration of a right to difference, as if this "right" were not already inherent to the law of life, which is to say, the insolvable violence, or yet in other words, the insurgency against its own alienation.

A right to difference that is content to repeat its claim without calling itself into question and without working on the active and reactive sites of its insurgency, this right here does not constitute a transgression. It is the parody of transgression, the parody of a life and a death that would be taken from us, behind our backs, against all crazy defiance. Then, to survive without weighing or knowing the consequences, therein lies the irreparable.

If therefore the West inhabits our innermost being, not as an absolute and devastating exteriority, nor as an eternal dominion, but really as a difference, a conglomerate of differences to be placed as such in every thought of difference and wherever it may come from; if therefore the West (thus named and thus situated) is not the reaction to an uncalculated distress, then everything remains to be thought—silent questions that endure in us.

Everything remains to be thought in dialogue with the most radical thoughts and insurgencies that have shaken the West and still do, in ways themselves different. Let us look straight away at what is *realized* before us and try to transform it according to a double critique—that of this Western legacy and of our very theological, very charismatic, and very patriarchal heritage. Double critique—we believe only in the revelation of the visible, the end of all celestial theology, and mortifying nostalgia.

Other-thought—that of nonreturn to the inertia of the foundations of our being. Here *Maghreb* designates the name of this gap, this nonreturn to the model of its religion and theology (no matter how well-disguised they may be under revolutionary ideologies), a nonreturn that can shake, in theory *and* in practice, the foundations of Maghrebi societies in their yet unformulated constitution by the critique that should disrupt it. This other-thought is posed before the great questions that shake our world today, where the planetary deployment of the sciences, techniques, and strategies makes way.

That is why here the name "Arab" is, on the one hand, the name of a civilization that is finished in its founding metaphysical element. "Finished" does not mean that this civilization is in reality dead, but that it is incapable of renewing itself as thought, except through the insurgency of an other-thought, which is dialogue with planetary transformations. On the other hand, the name "Arab" designates a war of naming and ideologies, which bring to light the active plurality of the Arab world.

Plurality and diversity, to which we shall return—with respect to the subversive element of an other-thought. For the unity of the Arab world is a thing of the past, if it is considered from the theocratic point of view of the "Ummah," an ideal matrix community of believers on earth. Therefore, this unity is, for us, of the past, to be analyzed in its imaginary insistence. And besides, this alleged unity that is claimed so vehemently includes not only its specific margins (Berber, Coptic, Kurdish ... and the margin of margins: the feminine), but also covers the division of the Arab world into countries, peoples, sects, and classes—and the divisions of divisions, up until the suffering of the individual, deserted by the hope of his god, forever invisible.

This division of the Arab world and being is not radically assumed. It is lived as such, between the nostalgia for a totalizing identity and a still formless, nonelaborated, in a word, unthought difference.

Yes, to look for something else in the division of the Arab and Islamic being, and to give up the obsession with the origin, with celestial identity and servile morality. To look for another thing and in another way—according to a plural thought—in the shaking of any beyond, whatever its determinations. The other, which would not be the being of transcendence, but the dissymmetrical eccentricity of a gaze and of a face-to-face—in life, and in death, without the help of any god.

This alterity—or this dissymmetrical eccentricity—is capable of shaking the metaphysics of a world still sustained by the order of theology and of a strong tyranny. No, we do not want to be its leftovers in the end of this century, if we consider this end in its process of devastation and naked survival.

Only the risk of a plural thought (with several poles of civilization, several languages, several technical and scientific elaborations) can, I think, assure for us the turning of this century on the planetary scene. And there is no choice—not for anyone. The transmutation of a world without return to its entropic foundations.

Fanon's call, in its very generosity, was the reaction of the humiliated during the colonial era, which is never done with decolonizing itself, and his critique of the West (in his *The Wretched of The Earth*, the book that remained unfinished until just before his death) was still caught in resentment and in a simplified Hegelianism—in the Sartrean manner. And we are still asking ourselves: Which West are we talking about? Which West opposed to ourselves, in ourselves? Who is "ourselves" in decolonization?

Yet "we" who grew politically during the emergence of the Third World, we who belong to this decolonial generation, we are no longer fooled by such a challenge nor tormented by the pangs of this unhappy consciousness. For centuries, we have believed too much in idols and gods to be still able to believe in men. That is why we believe in nothing. This means that this realization (let us keep calling it that by granting it its disillusioned—which is to say, affirmative in its incomplete transformations—truth), this realization of an intractable difference (see below), remains open to all temptation of the unthought in us and especially to the reproduction of what the West would develop according to its own will, as if, extending this alien will, we had become the chained and unleashed slaves in a tremendous system of repetition.

We were so young compared to the world's development, so vague in the face of the rigor of thought, and perhaps we had renounced many times a defenseless freedom, an unarmed thought (our only fate) given over to its real poverty.

When we talk of this Maghrebi generation of the sixties and focus our attention on the political considerations of the time, retrospectively, we find ourselves torn between Third-Worldist nationalism and dogmatic Marxism in the French manner. It should be borne in mind that in that regard we never accepted that the French Communist Party, with which we sympathized then, was so slow to understand the Algerian liberation movement, and through this event, the emergence of a politics whose ideological basis escaped it. This example of dogmatism is one among many, but apart from Marxism, no revolutionary theory seemed effective to us on a national and global level.

This critical inadequacy was worse than we thought, both on our side and on the side of the French left. For the conflict between Europe and the Arabs being age-old, it became, with time, a machine of mutual incomprehension. In order to be brought to light, this incomprehension required, and requires, an other-thought, independent of the political discourses of our time. What had we done, if not reproduce a simplified thought of Marx and, correspondingly, the theological ideology of Arab nationalism? But these two ideologies, and each on its own ground, are held by a moral and intellectual metaphysical tradition, whose conceptual edifice demands on our part a radical elucidation. We have failed before the exigency of this task. But this failure, which also has its regenerative forces, must be put into an other-strategy, which puts nothing forward without turning *against* its foundations—a strategy without a closed system, but which would be the construction of a game of thinking and the political, silently gaining ground against its failures and sufferings. To decolonize oneself is this *chance* of thought.

Some of us fell and gave into the servitude of the day; others continue to maintain, at all costs, the militant political task that is necessary within the framework of a party, a trade union, or a more or less secret organization. Others are dead or continue to survive the inflicted torture. But who among us—groups or individuals—has undertaken the effectively decolonizing work in its global reach of deconstituting the image we make of our domination, both exogenous and endogenous? We are still at the dawning of global thought. But we have grown up in the suffering that calls for the power of the word and revolt. If I told you, whoever you are, that this work has already begun and that you can hear me only as survivor, maybe then you will listen to the slow and progressive march of all the humiliated and all the survivors.

I call "Third World" this tremendous energy of surviving in transformation, this plural thought of survival whose duty is to live in its extraordinary freedom, a freedom without any final solution; but then, who ever said that the "end of the world" is in the hands of this technical and scientific system that plans out the world by subjecting it to the self-sufficiency of its will? Who ever claimed that new civilizations are not already at work, where everything seems inert, dead, flimsy, and absurd? Let us let all these professors of self-sufficiency proclaim the end of gods, the end of men, and the end of ends. Let us leave them to their self-sufficiency. We have lost too much and we have nothing to lose, not even the nothing. Such is the vital economy of an other-thought, which would be a gift bestowed by the suffering that seizes its terrible freedom.

On the margin

The thought of the "we" to which we turn no longer stands and no longer moves within the circle of (Western) metaphysics, nor according to the theology of Islam, but at their margin—*a margin on alert.*

On the planetary scene, we are more or less marginal, minoritarian, and dominated. They call it "underdeveloped." This is our very chance, the exigency of a transgression to declare and uphold constantly against any self-sufficiency. Moreover, a thought that is not inspired by its own poverty is always elaborated in order to dominate and humiliate; a thought that is not *minoritarian, marginal, fragmentary, and incomplete* is always a thought of ethnocide.

This—and I say with extreme caution—is not a call for a philosophy of the poor and for its glorification, but a call for a plural thought that does not reduce the others (societies and individuals alike) to the sphere of its self-sufficiency. To disappropriate oneself of such a reduction is, for all thought, an invaluable chance. This gesture—tremendous in its effects—challenges all thought that takes its particular scene for a planetary one, which is everywhere full of margins, gaps, and silent questions.

The "we" that I mention is this act of unsettling that is original and unthought in the face of all tyranny. The thought of this "we" is this *historial* linking that weaves being and that being weaves—at the margin of metaphysics. We should understand metaphysics as the representation of gods-become-men, the representation of the idea of god embodied in that of man. And in metaphysics, man has always been a "white" man, bearer of the light and its solar concepts. We cannot deserve our life and our death without the mourning of metaphysics. It is this mourning that urges us to pose otherwise the question of the repressed traditions.

Our problem is not traditional because it turns to these traditions, but it is not inactual[2] enough (in its very actuality) with respect to the dominant thoughts of today to understand, for instance, the (historical) retreat of the Arabs and their decline as a universal civilization, as an "intermediate civilization." S. D. Goitein writes, "We have called this civilization *intermediate*, because it is intermediate in *time* between Hellenism and Renaissance, intermediate in *character* between the largely secular culture of the later Roman period and the thoroughly clerical world of Medieval Europe, and intermediate in *space* between Europe and Africa on the one hand and India and China on the other thus forming for the first time in history a strong cultural link between all parts of the ancient world."[3]

This civilization went into a spectacular downfall starting from the fourteenth century. What happened? It will be necessary to resume the dialogue with the "intermediate" question of *this retreat and this decline toward the West.* A retreat that is more than ever active in every problematic of decolonialism. How to think this retreat in a precise manner? What about this retreat in the mourning of metaphysics? And it is not I who will contradict Friedrich Nietzsche when he declares, "Christianity has cheated us out of the harvest of ancient culture; later it cheated us again, out of the harvest of the culture of *Islam*. The wonderful world of the Moorish culture of Spain, really more closely related to *us*, more congenial to our senses and tastes than Rome and Greece, was *trampled down* (I do not say by what kind of feet). Why?

Because it owed its origin to noble, to male instincts, because it said Yes to life even with the rare and refined luxuries of Moorish life... . Later the crusaders fought something before which they might more properly have prostrated themselves in the dust—a culture compared to which even our nineteenth century might feel very poor, very 'late.' To be sure, they wanted loot; the Orient was rich. One should not be prejudiced. Crusades—higher piracy, nothing else!" (Cf. *L'Antéchrist*).[4]

Yes: theology, higher piracy. Yet this enthusiasm of Nietzsche and his settling of accounts must be situated in the great war he waged against Christianity and all theology. And we are *also* Muslims by tradition, which changes the strategic position of our critique.

Every reading or rereading of our heritage (*turath*) and every gaze cast at this glory of the past can have a decisive value for us only as a *lever* to a double critique.

That is why, when we engage in dialogue with Western thoughts of difference (the thought of Nietzsche, of Heidegger, and among our close contemporaries, the thought of Maurice Blanchot and Jacques Derrida), we take into account not only their style of thought but also their strategy and machinery of war in order to put them to the service of our cause, which is necessarily another conspiracy of the mind, requiring an effective decolonization and a concrete thought of difference.

On retreat

— Before you go on, we want to express our concern about the direction of your words. What metaphysics are you referring to so enthusiastically? What theology? Are you talking (if we grant that you are talking) on the basis of your tradition? On what theoretical ground? We are wondering whether the questions you raise are not in themselves veiled by the language you are writing?

— None of all this was given to me as grace, not even my tradition. But we mustn't lose from sight your first objection, which I make mine,

if we are aiming at the same thing. Of what metaphysics does it look
like we are talking? It is a matter of a face-to-face still unthought of: a
face-to-face of Western (basically Greek) and Islamic metaphysics,
as two radical formulations of Being, the One and the Whole. Let
us make ourselves clear: at the source of the Islamic word arises
the revelation of a language declared inimitable (*i'jaz*)—the Arabic
language. The metaphysical site par excellence, the Arabic language
brings together in the mind of the believer the visible and the
invisible, the present and the absent, earth and heaven.
— Also the Quran opens to him the gates of paradise.
— In it, the mystic will find his hallucinations as he passes through its
beatitudes and mortifications, ecstasy of the Book-become-god: the
word "transfiguration." Now, the hierarchy of the visible and the
invisible separates the body of the believer from his life and his
death, concrete and incalculable for all theology and in all its forms
(dialectic, negative, mystical). To give you an image, let us say that
no god will henceforth attend our death, no angel, and no demon
either. Our subversion—we have developed it elsewhere—is to
bring down heaven and hell in an other-thought, facing only the
visible.
— Perhaps, but let us stay right where the consciousness of this
absolute of the inimitable language is permeated by a miraculous
advent: the Quran.
— Yes, the Quran: simulacrum of the divine.
— Veiling the invisibility of Allah.
— The path you seem to be following is Greek, radically Greek: the
thought of the divine as presence of Being, as coming to pass,
etc. Have you read Heidegger in German, translating—in his
own way—the Greeks? And then, has it not been said over and
over again (are you illiterate or amnesic?) that Arabic philosophy
(as well as all philosophy that bears this name) is Greek in
essence?
— Yes, according to a certain direction of thought. I would say bluntly,
for example, that the God of Aristotle entered Islam before the

arrival of the latter. The theology of Islam and its global episteme
were preceded by Aristotle who preexists them. Would this
theology of Islam first be a *translation*? The translation into Arabic
of Abrahamic monotheism via Syriac and Greek? This research
perspective would be more accurate based on a *historial* dimension.

— We would understand better why the Arabs had invented the
famous *Theology* of Aristotle in order to erase, as it were, Greek
paganism and to circumvent Greek thought by the circle of
monotheism.

— Don't forget, these Arabs had a gift for inventing nice stories.

— Would theology be a divine fairytale?

— The fact you refer to (the apocryphal *Theology* of Aristotle) is
certainly an indicative anecdote; but, *you see*, it is the following stasis
that now seems absurd to me: Islam, which is the metaphysics of an
invisible god, lost its gaze in this face-to-face with the Greeks. Let
us not forget that Islam *veils* the face of women too, since the *houris*
cannot be seen *here below* except in the mystical paradise, isn't it
so? That is to say, in a hallucination of the visible? Thus, within this
hierarchy of the visible and the invisible, woman is placed between
God and man—visible invisible, she is the *mise en abyme* of the
theological order. Who ever kept you from working in this direction?

— But let us come back to this lost gaze and this splitting of God in
Arab philosophy. Our hypothesis is that the Arabs, in considering
the question of being on the basis of their *language*, carried out
a double translation via Syriac and Greek. Through this double
translation, a metaphysics of the Text was reinforced—hence the
modernity of a certain classical knowledge about the questions of
the sign, and the written sign in particular. But what developed
with remarkable strength is, don't forget, the great Islamic
mysticism as the ecstatic unity of God, the Text and Islam. We have
reached here a place where the invisible emerges in the visible, and
the absence of Allah is resorbed in a mortifying experience: the
hypostatized unity of a body-become-corpse offered to God, to the
Text and to Love.

— Let us curb your enthusiasm. You sometimes speak of the Arabs
as "they." Do you come from another planet? Where do you live
then? Or did you, like some Orientalists, fabricate another sort of
invisible Arabs, forever lost in the return of the dead?

— Promise to oneself—be infinitely Arab by excess.

— Or by default, as they say.

— Even.

— Were you suggesting that the Arabs are changing face?

— Insofar as the face of thought, withdrawn, starts looking at the
in-itself-distant other: the thought of being and of the desert, of
mystical passion, of the unity of Allah, the Text and Love. These
(now repressed) themes of today's traditional Arab thought should
be accommodated by our double critique.

— But this return is claimed by traditionalists as well.

— Traditionalism has lost the sense of tradition, the one we are aiming
at and which has identified the extreme limits of Arabic thought.
The *Salafi* (so-called Islamic fundamentalism) call for a certain
interpretation of *asala* (originarity) falls under a very questionable
reformist doctrine. This doctrinaire aim is to make of the Arabs a
people of political theologians, in an irreversibly other world.

— In countries where humiliation and poverty reign, you call upon
ghosts. Who are you talking to?

— We are defending the double critique and the intractable difference
of which, if you don't mind, we shall talk further below. But we
can take a step and make progress by keeping our attention on the
unthought of our extreme (in every sense of the word) past. There
is no return in itself, nothing, nothing but critical transformations,
from our perspective.

Three transformations

Now the Maghreb as horizon of thought emerges on the basis of three
transformations—three major features:

- *Traditionalism.* We call traditionalism *metaphysics reduced to theology.* Theology designates here the thought of the One and of the being as the first being, first cause, and so forth. In nonphilosophical terms, theology is the impossible science of God and of the origin of the world.
- *Salafism.* We call Salafism *metaphysics-become-doctrine.* Doctrine designates here the morality of a political conduct, of a social pedagogy, which would also be the reconciliation of science with religion, technology with theology.
- *Rationalism* (political, culturalist, historicist, sociologist, and so on). We call rationalism *metaphysics-become-technology.* Technology designates here the ordering of the world according to a new will to power, drawing its strength from scientific development.

Metaphysics that has become theology, doctrine, and technology—these three transformations can be approached, for instance, through history and sociology. Thus, for a Moroccan ideologist, Abdallah Laroui, the distinction between a cleric, a politician, and a technophile is as follows: "In contemporary Arab ideology we can identify three ways of grasping the essential problem in Arab society: the one locates it in religion, the other in political organization, and the last in scientific and technical activity."[5]

Such distinctions are indeed useful for psycho-ideological analysis, but only slightly do they touch upon the global question of the Arab world. Why so? Between religion, politics, and technology, there are *structural solidarities* that must be explained when one analyzes the Arab world as a whole. Solidarities, which clearly make themselves visible—metaphysics, theology, and morality, which continue to hold a major influence, cover the structures of Arab societies. And in any case, these questions are already tackled by Western thought that has gone further in the critique of ideologies, and what Laroui merely and above all retains from them is a certain historicism and a so-called "objective" Marxism. What West does he engage in dialogue with, supposing there is dialogue? And from what theoretical place does he talk, established at a distance between what he calls the West and the Arabs? We will see below that his propositions are immediately tautological.

What is at stake today and has been from the start is not simply the empiricist portrait of a certain "contemporary Arab ideology," but rather the *historial* destiny of the Arabs, their expansion and their decline, the chiasmus which ties them to the world (Western or other), as this destiny, since the dawn of Islam, is still there. The historical is not the *historial*, the ideological is caught in metaphysics, and the contemporary is turned toward the return of the Same *and* beyond all metaphysics. The question of the Arabs remains suppressed, and a radical critique remains open.

From the very beginning of philosophy in Islam (Al-Kindi), metaphysics is present as thought of being and of the being, as thought of substance, of the one and the many. This philosophy—following in the footsteps of the Greeks—in a way "lifts up" the speculative theology of *kalam*, a crucial point of which revolved around the creation or noncreation of the divine word. The retreat of this philosophy (from the thirteenth century onward) remains unthought: how to articulate this question, here and now? Today, so casually is the philosophy of the divine declared dead. Is it not necessary to first look closely at how Arab identity, claimed so vehemently today, continues to be fascinated by the sacral law? And the figure of the symbolic, which is to say the prophetic Father?

The date we give to the retreat may be considered otherwise when we refer to a properly mystical ontology, such as the ontology of Mulla Sadra who lived from 1572 to 1640.[6] What seems essential to us, through the question of the modern Arab and Muslim renaissance, is its relationship with decadence, for which we have two exemplary witnesses. Ibn Khaldun was the first to offer an explanation of this decadence, and Al-Ghazali who, despite his mystical anxieties, fought philosophy with the weapons of mysticism and mysticism with those of theology. Al-Ghazali is not just one theologian among others; he drove the classical Arab episteme to its theological limits. In other words, he barred the path to all autonomous rationality. He was in a way the legislator of the decadence.

When we criticize attempts such as Laroui's it is not for polemical reasons, but because it is possible for us to show (very easily) that this truth of historicism is nothing but a theological artifice in ideological form. We will demonstrate this later on two occasions. We are talking of the debate in its *historial* dimension (expansion, retreat, pinnacle, and rupture in every question of being); for, from a historical point of view, Laroui's work is itself a document, the specimen of an unthought decadence, which does not take charge in its repressed content, that is to say, in the relationship of history to metaphysics. Today who can claim that the techniques and the sciences, as well as the ideologies accompanying them, are not still a matter of the language or rather the *languages* of metaphysics? Nobody, not even the most vigilant psychoanalysis, and still less and on another level, systems science that we keep hearing about. We are told that this systematic whole is the totalizing construction of all the systems of thought, metaphorically, like Russian dolls connected to each other by some magic of the systemic scientist, universal speculator, and architect of the world in its scientific globality. What then is a system of systems, which is not already worked out by the organic unity of a metaphysical totality?

This is a necessary remark in order to briefly point out the naiveté of this sort of ideology that claims a historicism detached from the language of metaphysics and its notions of truth and science. Naiveté of this ideology—for instance, Arab philosophy knew, in its own way, what we are learning now in the West. We have forgotten the basics of the question of being and of the being, of identity and of difference, and we continue to chatter with no sense of decency on the recovery of identity and on the Arab renaissance. But reborn to what? To be reborn to thought is the memorable fate of ghosts, of the dead who talk to us and of the living who talk behind our backs. What amnesia! To speak is the critical transformation of life, of death, and of survival, while metaphysical thought is a system of cruelty that has tamed us into a servile morality.

This is our "theoretical" position, sustained from day to day by the suffering of experience, with respect to the repressed on which we put our finger. As a society, we are traditionalist by the forgetting of tradition, doctrinaire by the forgetting of the thought of being, and technophile by servitude. Who has *tamed* us such that this forgetting has become secular?

But forgetting is not nothingness, and neither is it abandonment outside of time; it is sustained by an active moral law, a ferocious theological intensity. Traditionalism is this activity, this hard work of punishment and restraint. It has not been said enough that the profound desire of the traditionalist is to take the place of God, eternal and unchanging. It is not surprising that he should eventually take refuge in the pure heaven of speculation! But as believer, he is a survivor. And he could always repeat, in his anguish, the words of the prophet Muhammad, according to which Islam would have come to exile on this earth and would disappear as alien. Yet, perhaps, deep down, this believer awaits an apocalypse, which would make him see with his own eyes the end of this world that has become more and more absurd and incomprehensible. *Apocalypse now*, we would say, in all thought that seizes its terrible freedom. That is why we call the sad figure of this survivor, "traditionalist."

Traditionalism, as we have said, is not tradition; it is the forgetting of tradition, and as forgetting, it ties ontology to this dogma: primacy of a Being (God) that is unchanging and eternal, invisible and absent. However, this dogmatic and deadly can take place, in our age, only in the realm of an in-itself disenchanted world, favorable to the unhappy consciousness and perpetual suffering. Traditionalism feeds on the hatred of life. Eating itself up, century after century, it falls over into monstrosity and devilry. Theology is now, and more and more, a perverted doctrine of evil and cruelty. And let us not forget that God can drive you crazy, which is interesting for all demonic thought and for all thought of madness. That is why the traditionalist now turns to mysticism, that is to say, to a degraded form of the great Islamic mysticism, which belongs to an ecstatic experience of being, incapable now of forming the crux of an other-thought. To be more precise, when I engage in dialogue with this mysticism, it is not because of nostalgia of the return, but because of the transmutation of its ordeal. For mysticism is a divine torture, while we suffer from an other-thought of all torture. And what suffers in the Arab being is the survival of God.

For its part, Salafism seeks to go beyond traditionalism. Its will is doctrinaire—to reform the moral decay of the world and its corruption (cf. for instance, in Morocco, the doctrinaire studies of Allal al-Fassi). However, neither traditionalism nor Salafism can surpass itself by its own energy. Why? Because in losing their way in the contemporary world, they are capable neither of returning against their theocratic foundations nor of making a leap of thought, that is to say, engaging in dialogue with the outside (evil) that impairs them by destroying them from within. This outside and this evil are considered as the effects of Western domination and the loss of faith. Yet, alterity is dissymmetry of all identity (individual, social, cultural)—I am always an other and this other is not you, meaning, a double of my self. Who suffers in me if not this other! And this other is constitutive of my ontological separation, my pain in the world.

On the doctrinaire level, however, Salafism thinks that it adapts (Western) techniques to theology, by a double economy:

- an economy of means: according to Salafism, technology would be an instrument that can be integrated into Islamic societies, without this supposed integration calling into question the social structure that sustains Salafism and the social structure of the Arab world;
- an economy of ends: technology is also assumed to be stripped of the values that institute it. Therefore, it would be possible for the Salafi doctrine to master and control it according to its own aims, already codified by religion. Needless to say, evolution that is increasingly imposed by technology is impregnable in this doctrinaire project. And if, since the middle of the nineteenth century, Salafism continues to run idle without founding new societies, it is because theology, in its project of regeneration, must devastate itself.

Yes, and what about rationalism, as claimed by the Maghrebis? This introduction is not a global study of all the scientific disciplines, as they are practiced in these countries. Here the reader will find the critique of other discourses (sociological, ethnological, Orientalist) and of their application to the analysis of Maghrebi societies. For the time being, we shall continue to focus our mind on just one example prevailing in the Maghreb within "the human sciences," namely, historicism.

Every society, in writing its own history, writes the time of its rooting; and through this gesture, it projects onto the past that which, in the present, remains concealed. Yes, history is the question of this concealment and the germination of its multiple identity. And if there is "history" for us, it will have always existed: in the future perfect. But let us listen to the other voice.

"Let us make generalized historicism," such is Abdallah Laroui's watchword. No doubt, this historicist had the merit of wanting to reread "historical consciousness" against Arab and, in particular, Maghrebi ideology. He insists on the sense of continuity, the necessary historical continuity; he insists on the long-term method in order to situate the colonial situation and our "cultural retardation" (the expression is his) within a global historical field, and introduce in local historiography an ideological critique divested of certain Orientalist prejudices. Laroui denounces "the dispossession of the subject" through the research made in the colonial era or through traditionalism and Salafism that freeze Arab history in a past yearning for the initial model.

All these efforts are useful and necessary, and they constitute a first stage of decolonizing analysis. But the *historial* question (the question of the peak and the decline, the question of the future perfect of all history) is reduced to a generalized historicism that threatens nothing but its own theoretical impasse. Why? Laroui reduces history and its concept to a metaphysical totality, enclosed by continuity, rationality, and the truth of what history would be, as if "the subject of history" were an absolute and transparent reason, not only in its unfolding, but also in the biography of the historian—and as if, from the individual subject to the historical subject, there were not a "translation" of the narrative of the unconscious. All that I can tell is perhaps only a more or less sensible transposition, an association that is more or less free of facts, events, and ideas, which, without my biography, would have remained silent in my archeology. What about the historical subject apart from the narrative of the unconscious? History—an optical illusion. Yes, but the illusion of a metaphysical representation, as long as it speaks in the name of truth and objectivity.

Furthermore, in seeking to explain history chiefly by continuity, Laroui lets the other—equally active—gesture slip through his fingers: the gesture of the gap, of discontinuity, disorder, and dissymmetry. In the violence of (historical) being, there is always a loss, a nonreturn. And it is this loss, this monstrosity of the immemorial, that conceals, by calling for *historial* thought, our access to it.

Let us clarify. Laroui attempts to engage in dialogue with Marxism, a certain Marxism under Hegel's thought. Yet in one of its most rigorous forms (Althusser), Marxism "repudiates":

- transcendental historicism (of the theocratic society) defined by absolutes (God, Prophecy, Fatality);
- historicism of liberal thought (eighteenth-century Europe) that replaced the absolutes of transcendence with the now-secularized substitutes, which are Reason, the Individual, Freedom. The metaphysical ground remains the same, but there is an ideological shift, a critical transformation.

Nothing obliges us Arabs to take the same path and go through once again the same stages as did the Marxist West for its own part. From the outset, one must start from what *is*, from what is here and now as a question, a provocation, a challenge to thought. Althusser, for instance, reclaimed history, the class struggle as a trial without subject or finality; he thus changes the theoretical position of Marxism by surpassing the two historicisms aimed at here. Laroui's work, precisely, remains enclosed between the two, which means that it is a matter of a surpassed historicism.

What is *necessary* (the duty of an other-thought) is to broaden our freedom to think, to introduce in all dialogue several strategic levers—for example, to eliminate from discourse the absolutes of theology and theocentricism, which shackle the time, space, and edifice of Maghrebi societies. But this is not enough. The dialogue with all thought of difference is monumental. It aims to unsettle all that stupefies us in repetition and reproduction. An other-thought is always a plot, a conspiracy, a perpetual revolt, and a relentless risk. And we are so defenseless in the face of the power of the world. Such is our "history," which will have struck the body.

To shake up, through a vigilant critique, the order of dominant knowledge (wherever it comes from) is to introduce thought into the current social and political struggle. But such a struggle has its forgotten inactuality, toward which one must move with the energy of *historial* being, in this world held by an irresistible will to power.

What ruins Laroui's historicism is his loyalty to a naïve interrogation of being, since he speaks constantly of identity without grasping the philosophical and metaphysical stakes involved. This is how Laroui confuses "the Other" with "the others" and "other people," and cultural anthropology with the thought of difference. Besides, these "different" propositions about Arab being cancel themselves: we do not need to exaggerate their naiveté. Already in the first paragraph of the first chapter on "contemporary Arab ideology," he writes, "For three quarters of a century, the Arabs have been asking themselves the one and same question: who is the other and who is I?"[7] As if this was not the question of being since the beginnings of human language, let alone philosophical language. By which "historicist" detour does Laroui forget the question of being and the being, of the identical and the different, as it is posed in Greek and Arab philosophy? Laroui's ideology is, from the outset, ruined. But it will be objected that a historian does not have to refer to philosophy. I do not know what history a historian can practice if not the history of the languages that translate the facts, the events, and all the traces to be deciphered. And if what he seems to discover no longer holds any

secrets for a philosopher of the fifth century before the Gregorian age,
I consequently do not see the important use of such studies on Arab
identity and ideology.

On intractable difference

— You speak of technology in a tendentious manner. At times, you
  seem to reduce it to a demonic fatality.
— We have said it many times—technology is neither good nor bad.
  It is, of course, a universal destiny of science! No society resists
  its expansion—can it be stopped, the development of the world?
  Wherever humankind gains a foothold, technology is already there,
  as a second dwelling.
— Which means that it is everywhere, regardless of the society.
— Yes, of course. Let's take the case of Morocco. We import machines;
  we import so-called development models. These models can be
  more or less effective and adaptable.
— They may sometimes help to reduce some poverty. A certain level
  of economic growth may be attained on the basis of more or less
  accurate planning.
— Accurate to the extent that the human body is itself a reservoir
  of calculable work—its quality of life and survival, of procreation
  and death.
— What happens to these imported machines and models?
— They create an image, a split representation of their system of
  origin. Also, they produce local technocracies that take care of
  their management. This cumulative effect is, in itself, unlimited.
  We don't see the end of it. With these machines and these models,
  we import a certain relation of man with his kind, of man
  with being.
— Can such an ontological relation be imported?
— We would like to talk of a simulacrum of technology.
— What do you mean?

— Well, let's take up very quickly the great Heideggerian question on technology as "completed metaphysics." You know how much this thinker was tormented by this question as I formulate it here.

— How is this torment ours?

— We would say, following Heidegger, that technology as "completed metaphysics" and as will to power is the proclamation of an unprecedented planetary warning that calls man—more than ever—to listen to Being, and to a thought of difference. If we want to mark an active specificity, for the time being, we cannot skip over this thought of difference, which is not the only one, whatever may be the critical gesture to oppose it.

— And yet Heidegger insisted too much on the devastation of the world, on the fate of man becoming a beast of burden, and a number manipulated by computers.

— There is a wealth of signs that confirm this torment. Look around you! Look in you! Poetry has become a technical exercise. An "avant-garde" author recently declared that he desired to write like a computer, and moreover, we have seen so-called artistic productions created by computers. This expansion of technology is universal. That is why, and regardless of our position on these mechanical games, technology is not an evil, but a question on the meaning of being.

— Yes, if we accept these propositions on the relationships between metaphysics and technology. But let us go back to what ties *us* to an essence of technology (and we should rather talk of *techniques*). After all, technology is a dominating and imperial will to power, since it is at the disposal of the powers of its holders. It is, in a way, the completion of Absolute Knowledge, as systemized by Hegel. Could we bend this tremendous will to power to our advantage?

— Our advantage? We? Who are we, in this question? We, in the deployment of technology? The East is not a simple (dialectical, speculative, culturalist) movement toward the West. They are for each other the beginning and the end. And we are trying to go toward a planetary and plural thought, this other-thought, that

is built step by step and without a certain end. That is why the
Hegelian metaphor of the two suns (the outer sun of the East and
the inner sun of the West as universal thought) is still caught in
metaphysics. And this is to take just one example in Hegel's gigantic
system, without which the world is even more incomprehensible.
— What does this metaphor mean for your understanding of
technology and its simulacrum?
— The essence of technology is unique. And being unique, it is
universal, irrespective of the mode of its deployment. The unique
has its effects of dissimulation, as fold, refold, and differentiation.
We call this whole scene "the simulacrum of technology."
— Which means?
— The essence of technology is split with respect to the metaphysical
ground of Islam and its values. We were saying earlier that the God
of Aristotle entered Islam before Islam appeared. The same is true
for his *organon*, prelude to the universal destiny of technology. That
is why we must focus our attention on the face-to-face of these
two metaphysics, with the one erasing the other. We are caught in
this gap, in an as yet unprecedented gesture. It is not in order to
reread these traditions infinitely that we thus speak, but in order to
provoke a crisis, to put ourselves into crisis within the unthought of
that which is our lot, or rather within this necessity to differentiate
oneself. Difference is not granted to the first rebel.
— So this is what you call "intractable difference."
— Yes. And there are other gaps, other ruptures that are unleashed
in the violence of some against the others. In the Arab world, the
machinegun is at the end of theology like a sinister unleashing of
metaphysics. You have examples of this everywhere in the Arab and
the Iranian world. The intractable difference is a relinquishment
of metaphysics by a double critique, a double combat, and a
double death.
— Double critique, you say?
— Critique of these two metaphysics, and of their face-to-face. In fact,
there is no choice. We should think Maghreb as it *is*, topographical

site between the East, the West, and Africa, and such that it can
become global for its own account. In a way, this movement has
always been underway. But this *historial* movement necessitates an
accompanying thought. On the one hand, one should listen to the
Maghreb resonate in its (linguistic, cultural, political) plurality, and
on the other, only the outside rethought, decentered, subverted,
diverted from its dominant determinations, can allow us to go
beyond unformulated identities and differences. Only the outside
rethought—for our part—is able to break our nostalgia for the
Father and tear it away from its metaphysical ground—or at least,
to bend it toward such a tearing, toward this intractable difference
that takes itself in charge of its sufferings, its humiliations, and,
I would say, of its insolvable problems. Such is the other side of our
relationship to such a thought of difference; for originarity (*asala*[8])
with which they poison our minds is still a poison of theology,
which is a clever, a very clever stealer of minds enchanted by belief.
— Then what is the meaning of "double death"?
— Heraclitus said it in his enigmatic voice: "Immortal mortals, mortal
immortals, living the death of the others and dying their life."[9]
Human dignity is to be worthy of one's life and of one's survival
among the living and of one's death, one's natural death among the
dead, do you hear me?

(1981)

2

Double Critique

Philosophers: The world has no age. Humanity simply changes place.
You are in the Occident, but free to live in your Orient, as ancient as
you please, and to live well. Don't admit defeat. Philosophers, you are
of your Occident.[1]

Rimbaud (*The Impossible*)

This study consists of two parts: The first is on the decolonization of
sociology, while the other constitutes an analysis of the discourses of the
social, applied to a single example: *precolonial hierarchy in the Maghreb,*
and particularly in Morocco.

The first one written in 1974 was substantially revised for this
publication, while the second, which dates from 1970, is reproduced more
or less as it was. Here too the same angle is taken: the power of discourse
and the discourse of power. Actually, this is how one passes from one part
to the other: a relationship of structural solidarity and reversal.

An other-thought, analyzing itself in the words and laws that ground
and bear it, works to penetrate the question of nonpower on the one hand
and, on the other, to try to go beyond this opposition (power, nonpower)
toward a research that would erase itself at the margins of metaphysics.
This is what this dialogue aims for in its specific context.

I. Decolonization of sociology

From the viewpoint of what is still called the Third World, we cannot say
that decolonization has managed to promote a radically critical thought

vis-à-vis the ideological machine of imperialism and ethnocentrism—a decolonization that would at once be a deconstruction[2] of the discourses that contribute, in different and more or less hidden ways, to imperial domination, in this case understood equally in its power of speech. Yes, we have not reached this decolonization of thought that would be, beyond an overturning of this power, the affirmation of a difference, an absolute and free subversion. There is something of a gap there, a silent interval between the fact of colonization and that of decolonization. Not that subversive and responsible words do not pop up or develop here and there, but something stifled and almost lost does not manage to reach the speaking word, and to give itself this power and this risk.

Yet let us limit ourselves to the social, to sociology as it calls itself. Now like any sociology of decolonization (but what is it to be decolonized?), the sociology of the Arab world consists in carrying out a double task:

1. a deconstruction of logocentrism and ethnocentrism, this speech of self-sufficiency par excellence that the West, in the course of its development, developed on the world. And we have much to reflect—here on this side—on the structural solidarity that links imperialism in all its aspects (political, military, cultural) to the expansion of the so-called social sciences. A huge task, it is true: between the fact of colonization and that of decolonization, what is at stake is the destiny of science and technology as forces, energies of domination and mastership over the totality of the world, and the over world as well.
2. This equally presupposes, or rather necessitates, a critique of the knowledge and discourses elaborated by different societies of the Arab world about themselves.

The overturning of mastership, subversion itself, depends on this decisive act of turning infinitely against one's own foundations, one's origins, those origins undermined by the whole history of theology, charisma, and patriarchy, if one can characterize thus the structural and permanent givens of this Arab world. It is this abyss, this nonknowledge of our decadence and dependence that should be brought to light, named in its destruction and transformation beyond its possibilities somehow.

This double-faced critique is also the violence of an uprooting. Therefore, a double movement that is indissociable in its aim is, we think, the only one capable of opening up for the sociologists of these countries the possibility of a knowledge that is less reproductive and more adapted to their real difference, which is life itself.

Let us resume. What do we mean by deconstruction, or more precisely, by the deconstruction of concepts? A first level of approach (and here I refer to the indispensable works of Jacques Derrida and Michel Foucault) consists in extracting the constitution of concepts and their framework in accordance with the laws that govern them, from the outside to the inside, from what is social to intrinsic discourse. No researcher can escape the question of the archeology of this knowledge, which he means to exercise within the limits of his consciousness and his free speech. But the more consciousness plunges into its archeology, the more research comes up against a stratification of discursive masses and disparate events, masses that are coagulated and dispersed, as it were, in the rock of their foundations. It is from stratum to stratum that a deconstitution of knowledge to be criticized and deported toward a thought other than the edifice of an episteme draws itself endlessly toward its origins by moving away from them. The researcher is the double, the split being of this distancing, this uprooting, as long as he remains within this need to criticize himself while being erased in the object of analysis to be deconstituted. Such a distance and such an operation of the outside that sees itself working against the self-sufficiency of his reason and of the identity of the "I" can establish the terms of a contract that the researcher signs with his thinking possibilities, which is to say, a *blank contract* with the unthought. What would the social be from the archeological point of view, if not these scattered traces: institutions, laws, and counter-laws of all kinds? What would it be without this once-and-for-all completed disorganization, this anarchy of signs to be formed in the patient and painful education of consciousness, but while keeping this consciousness on the threshold of its silences? And there is an "archeology of silence" that cannot be shown by the social and its edifices except by a subversion sustained against them. In this sense, when we speak of underdeveloped societies, we should rather say "silent societies." Even as they speak, they are not heard in their difference. Are we destined to use violence against the others in order to make them hear the voice of reason? Must we threaten them with war, destruction, and horrible guilt so that the West turns against its self-sufficiency and its ethnocentrism, now raised to the planetary level? And yet we, the Third World, can take a third path: neither reason nor unreason as thought by the West as a whole, but a kind of double subversion that, by giving itself the power of speech and action, sets to work in an intractable difference. To be decolonized would be the other name of this other-thought, and decolonization would be the silent completion of Western metaphysics. And this is where begins this third speech, this unbinding of Western reason, in its sciences and techniques. How can this researcher bear in himself the Third World—which is a plural question—within a thought that must accept the overturn of all values and hierarchies? Insurgency is an exigency of life and of survival. Once again, there is no choice. Endless debate—let us make a leap.

Historically, the sciences of the social have developed in the West. This development is itself contemporary with imperialistic hegemony and the expansion of industries and technologies. Very well—this is an observation, not a question. We shall come back later, always later, to the implications of this planetary event with respect to the deconstruction of these sciences. For the time being, let us say that this observation would be of no interest to us if it did not call into question a structural solidarity between these sciences of the social as such on the one hand and Western societies in their industrial and imperial phase on the other. Yes, this has been said again and again. Nevertheless, let us put forward another argument. For instance, Marxism presents itself as, claims to be, and is practiced—in some way or another—against imperialism. But as a Western thought that has become universal; how does it analyze other societies? There is one detail that remains crystal clear, if not schematic: Marxism, in its traditional typology, groups together the other societies under the Asiatic mode of production. This is a general term, even too general, that encompasses a remarkable number of various societies and cultures. In a single precolonial society (Morocco), it is possible to distinguish several conflicting systems: the patriarchal system, the tribal system, artisanal and market capitalism, the rural seigniorial system, and the Makhzen (the State), which actually became dominant only after colonization, which means that its capacity to rule was reinforced thanks to the instruments and techniques of power bequeathed by imperialism. This is indeed historical logic. And let us not forget what Marx wrote about England's occupation of India: "England has to fulfill a double mission in India: one destructive, the other regenerating—the annihilation of old Asiatic society and the laying of the material foundations of Western society in Asia."[3]

A dreadful statement in its very nakedness, which deserves some thought. We are justified in asking ourselves what is the place of the Hindus with respect to this redeeming dialectic; those Hindus, of a superior and ancient metaphysics, and a rather exceptional thought on negativity and on death; those Hindus who, socially, do not conform to Marx's classification, but to a very singular system of caste and hierarchy.

We may therefore read Marx in the following manner: the tradition of the other must be murdered and its past liquidated so that the West, by taking over the world, can expand beyond its limits, only to remain the same in the end. The East must be shattered so that it comes back to the West, that is to say, to the metaphysics of the Same. The East must be separated from itself, severed in its continuity, and cut off from its time and its memory. Cut off from its time: where it must find itself in dialectical reason—in this case Hegelian, let us recall. This form of negation that is imperialism is therefore a regenerative power of the world to colonize, westernize, and "capitalize" to the extreme limit where it is reversed in the advent of communism. It is necessary to destroy, to regenerate: this is the principle that Marx's West imposes, and must impose on the other, on this rather strange India that, for thousands of years, has never ceased to pose enigmas.

It would be futile to suggest that Marx spoke ill of others and that this constitutes, in a way, a logical error of his system. We think that this system (for it is a system) should be questioned as a whole and with its remarkable weaknesses, that is, also with respect to its will to power that accompanied, while diverting it, the expansion of imperialism. An immense task, it is true, but inevitable for all other-thought that claims to rise on another ground than the West as a whole.

But let us quickly set aside this objection, which would reduce Marx's thought to a murderous ethnocentrism. Who can deny that he was against colonialism and imperialism? Again, who can deny that his thought has served and continues to serve the Third World for the overthrow of imperialism and local powers? It is another objection that we are raising against him, about this willpower that seeks to unite the world on the basis of a world system and of which the least that can be said is that it fails to recognize the other as such, in its irreducibility. In this sense, Marx's thought, more or less dissociable from Hegel's and therefore from Western metaphysics, has achieved an absolute form of Absolute Knowledge, in shaking up the world by way of an inexorable dialectic.

That is why this other-thought that we uphold is neither Marxist in the strict sense nor anti-Marxist in the right-wing sense of the word, but stands at the limits of its possibilities. For we seek to decenter in us Western knowledge, to decenter ourselves with respect to this center, this origin that the West gives itself. This should be done by operating already in the field of a plural and planetary thought, difference that struggles against its own reduction and domestication.

Let us go back to the sciences of the social. Since there is no sociology in itself, that is, detached from its cultural archeology, we may carry out the double critique put forward here. We need a scientific and ideological strategy, but also an active plurality of leashing and unleashing, violence and self-violence in all wars of repudiation.

Let us take an example illustrating this aspect of the double critique. Contemporary Arab knowledge cannot, without a radical rupture, escape its theological and theocratic foundations, which mark the ideology of Islam and of all monotheism. Thus, the task is to point the finger at the places where such knowledge is an *ideological adaptation* of metaphysical concepts, including Arab Marxist sociology. It is in this way that Arab sociologists or Orientalists use this notion—borrowed from Ibn Khaldun—of *asabiyyah* (socio-agnatic solidarity and solidarity of the political clientele, in a general way). Very well. Only, this notion implies a cyclical representation of history, in relation to the initial model, revelation of the Quran and of the prophecy of Muhammad. How can a dialectical thought assume a discourse situated between theology and a speculative dialectic? Would *asabiyyah* be transposable into that of the class struggle? The underlying debate that Maghrebi sociology cannot avoid here is that of the contradiction and the opposition between religious ontology and a historicist one, between an ideology based on theology and an ideology that considers social classes as the subject of history and of its transformations.

But perhaps what we see as a contradiction is actually a matter of *translation*. Let us clarify this point fully. It is time to take note of this testament (although written by no one): Ibn Khaldun has no heir. Or else, this heritage was indirectly taken up by Marx. Irony of history, indeed! Hence also these tireless efforts courageously made by certain Arab researchers in order to grant Khaldunian rationality to Marxist dialectics, in other words, to introduce continuity where there is difference, a yet unthought-of discontinuity, an outside that is irreducible from one language to another. Ibn Khaldun: a vestige! Yes, but what is a vestige, a remainder of thought that remains to be thought?

When we focus for a moment on the situation of Maghrebi sociology, we find ourselves faced with Ibn Khaldun, and with colonial and postcolonial sociology: three moments to be analyzed in their continuity and discontinuity. We do not want to return to what we have described elsewhere,[4] but let us simply recall a sentence by one of the ideologists of colonization, G. Hardy: "When one day the intellectual history of our colonial world is written—and what a history it will be, lively, ardent, colorful, rich, just like the military history of individual heroisms and braveries—we shall be surprised to observe, here and there, the irregularity, the discontinuity of production; and we shall witness, one after the other, magic blossomings and shrivellings from the sirocco, and the cause of these alternations of fertility and sterility will easily be found in the temperament of the men in power."[5]

Decolonize sociology? Certainly, but in a radical manner: subversion, the power of speech against the speech of power that seizes all society—this also *remains* to be shown on the level of analysis. All the work produced around the social by Maghrebis remains very often a reproduction or adaptation of this or that current sociological theory, without the primordial question of language being rigorously addressed therein.

Let us situate the problem in its metaphysical dimension and listen to these remarks by Derrida about ethnology:

> Now, ethnology—like any science—comes about within the element of discourse. And it is primarily a European science employing traditional concepts, however much it may struggle against them. Consequently, whether he wants to or not—and this does not depend on a decision on his part—the ethnologist accepts into his discourse the premises of ethnocentrism at the very moment when he denounces them. This necessity is irreducible; it is not a historical contingency. We ought to consider all its implications very carefully. But if no one can escape this necessity, and if no one is therefore responsible for giving in to it, however little he may do so, this does not mean that all the ways of giving in to it are of equal pertinence. The quality and fecundity of a discourse are perhaps measured by the critical rigor with which this relation to the history of metaphysics and to inherited concepts is thought. Here it is a question both of a critical relation to the language of the social sciences and a critical responsibility of the discourse itself. It is a question of explicitly and systematically posing the problem of

the status of a discourse, which borrows from a heritage the resources necessary for the deconstruction of that heritage itself. A problem of *economy* and *strategy*.[6]

Economy, strategy—also as part of the enunciation of the double critique. This allows us to distinguish, on the one hand, discourses, concepts (and chains of concepts) endowed with a potential that remains to be realized, and on the other, those that are to be classified within the history of knowledge. An archeological analysis is decisive for carrying out this strategy and this effective decolonization.

To Derrida's propositions we should add—as to our specific research—that the space of our speech and of our discourse is dual by virtue of our *bilingual situation*. When we allow ourselves to be confronted with two metaphysics (Western and Islamic: we should say two metaphysical forms, for metaphysics is *one*, being the metaphysics of the One, the Whole, and the Same), do we not run the risk of passing from one to the other without bringing to light the translation and the transportation that take place, imperceptibly, from one archeology to another and from one language to another? Certainly, this is the great risk involved. We would say this: in criticizing the ideology of Islam and Arab knowledge by means of a Western thought, opposing and confronting all metaphysics by means of an other-thought, we are thus exposed to a duplicity that must be explained in this approach of difference. Difference? It is this outside, this far-away that is never reached but always sensed, and yet present and active in life itself.

However, it will be said, is this possible? For in using the sciences of the West and their philosophical ground, you circulate in a set of thoughts that can only absorb you; and in this way you will facilitate the loss of the present Arab culture, or worse, a more powerful and subtle domination of this world. You fight against repetitive traditionalization or Westernization from a dangerous position that would relegate Arab knowledge to an ideological past. Would there be any future there? And what you call "double critique"? Is it not simply the strategy of every critique? Every critique is double: it deconstitutes the object of analysis by moving away from it, by setting other landmarks, and by paving other ways for its advancement. Are you not doing the same thing, by means of a game of doubles and a game of simulacrum, using in turn the East against the West, and the West against the East? Is this not a *sick duplicity*, which does not form, through its solitary effort, the constitution of an other-thought, absolutely and truly turned toward the unprecedented and the unsayable? Science and the sciences of the social of which you speak are immobilized in this infinite splitting, while to form a name, a genealogy, and laws that properly belong to an other-thought is an event that does not depend on any individual will. It is the very notion of language that should be overturned, made a stranger to itself. An impossible, superhuman power, madness of difference that wants to be intractable, irreducible, and without the stable support of its traditional foundations and its maternal language, here almost given over to silence.

Let us remove these concerns with respect to a single point. Let us say, by way of description, that current Arab knowledge is a conflicting interference between two epistemes, one of which (the Western) covers the other; it restructures the other from within, detaching it from its historical continuity. And this to such an extent that the Arab researcher, who is accustomed to Western knowledge, always risks not having an idea of the place from where he speaks, and where these problems tormenting him really come from.

Yes, but Arab knowledge maintains a certain autonomy, thanks to its native tongue. Hence its possibility for thinking and for thinking the other by translating it, by grafting it to this possibility, opening this possibility toward the unknown—the nonknowledge to think again and again between two or more languages.[7] This entry into globality through this transformation of the Arab language is probably the future of this knowledge, its accession to planetary speech, which is still, and to such an extent, an ethnocentric speech and a speech of self-sufficiency.

This situation, which should be approached in its different aspects, brings about a first remark. The Arab researcher essentially becomes the *translator* (more or less good) of a set of thoughts and of sciences formed elsewhere, and whose questions of archeology, most of the time, he hardly suspects. Frightened by the intellectual production of the West and by an accelerated accumulation process, this researcher remains content with constructing, in the *shadow* of the Western episteme, a secondary, residual knowledge that satisfies no one. Is this a simple situation of unknowing? No, the question is older and more fundamental: we must not forget that the Arabs, at the time of their initial confrontation with the Greeks, had to translate in order to establish an autonomous philosophical and scientific language! This language is a mark of the past, and what has remained is indeed theology (including *fiqh*); this theology—as the impossible science of an invisible god—still works according to the idea of a unique, sacred, and miraculous language, incapable of *speaking in tongues*. Yet translation requires a plurality of languages and thoughts, inscribing themselves therein. And an other-thought, such as we envisage it, is a *thought in tongues*, a globalizing translation of the codes, systems, and constellations of signs that circulate in the world and above (in a nontheological sense). Each society or group of societies is a relaying of this globalization. A strategy that does not actively work to transform these relays is, perhaps, condemned to eat itself and turn on itself—entropically.

Everything tumbles down (according to this perspective) as soon as we face up to the question of such a conflict, whether actual or inactual. When the Arab researcher focuses his attention on this accumulation process, he realizes the great necessity, the inescapable obligation to engage in dialogue with the totality of the Western and universal episteme. The more decisive the critical rupture is, the more it constitutes itself within a difference, within the unknown. So much so that all theory (for instance, sociological in this case) is a system of thought, produced by a differential history and an active plurality, provided that this history is considered (this has been repeated many times) not according to a linear movement (evolutionist or otherwise), but as the fabric of relations between series of events that draw their sole coherence from our mode of thinking and unthinking (cf. Nietzsche).

Everything remains to be done, in this second sense that these sciences of the social refer to fundamental notions (reason, truth, objectivity, science, culture, and nature), whose site remains held by a metaphysical language. To forget this thread that ties philosophy to science and ideology, and the whole to a thought of difference, is to insist on remaining within reproduction, within the work of mimesis. And yet, these observations that can be demonstrated—discourse by discourse—(from history to the most modern semiology) continue to circulate. In this sense, they are words of power.

Let us be clear: it is not a matter of activating or reactivating, in the place of the West, its internal critique, which is at work in a remarkable way on many levels of thought and speech. Current Western episteme is therefore put into crisis from within by forces of transcendence and decentering. This episteme presents itself to us, the Third World, according to variable modalities and figures, themselves formed within the struggle, the competition, the will to power, and a war of naming.

Taking a step back, a schematic one to tell the truth, we arrive at three modes of thought:

1. *institutional thoughts*, which legitimize ethnocentrism, while enunciating a speculative universalism and humanism (this is the speech of the legislator of the Western order);
2. *critical thoughts*, which introduce, into this episteme, a conceptual decentering, a shifting of the intellectual ground on which this episteme has been elaborated. Although they cannot escape the values of their culture (and how could they?), these thoughts take into account the differential gaps, the unthought-of plurality of societies, cultures, and eras of civilization. In short, they institute one thought of difference as the crux of their critique. This is the reversal of the speech of power into the power of speech;
3. *thoughts of the impossible*, whether it be a question of the unthought or of the unconscious. The extreme point of the will to power: these thoughts *want* to destroy themselves in their power

of speech, by turning against all institutions, including that of
thought in itself, be it the thought of difference and of identity, or
critical, constitutive and deconstitutive, affirmative and negative.
In other words, this vertiginous movement of the impossible (this
becoming mad of all thought and of all reason) is still a *question
of language*.

The same is true for the present Arab episteme. Its traditional
(classical) ground is a structural whole, which includes theology and
mysticism as well as scientific thoughts, including one particular
knowledge (which has been transformed): *al-adab*. The positivity
of these different knowledges corresponded to a civilization now
surpassed in its founding elements, although their discourses are
still very much alive. There are many, far too many Arab researchers
who work to read and reread this heritage (*turath*) that transforms
"documents into monuments" as Michel Foucault puts it. How to
situate this episteme?

Let us quickly decide: it is necessary to break with *patrimonialism*,
that is, this return to a past glory, depressing nostalgia, and never-
ending death. The double critique we have put forward finds here its
strategic lever:

> *First*: to perform a reduction of metaphysical language that derives
> from the two sources, the Western source and that of the Arab culture.
> We have insisted a great deal on this point, whilst suggesting that
> such a will to reduction can cancel itself out in its project, being itself
> reduced to empty rhetoric. Every will is at the limits of its possibility.
> But to explore the space of its possibility is already to give oneself the
> time to look for it, with no hope of redemption, in any way.

> *Second*: to deconstitute the structural solidarity of the Western
> episteme with respect to its different wills (imperialism, ethnocentrism,
> self-sufficiency).

The present Arab knowledge operates at the *margin* of the Western
episteme—therefore neither inside it, since it is rather subordinated to

and determined by it, nor outside, since it does not think the *outside* that grounds it. The margin is actually a blind limit. The double critique consists in opposing to the Western episteme its unthought-of outside, while radicalizing the margin, not only in a *thought in Arabic*, but also in an other-thought that speaks *in tongues*, listening to every word— from wherever it comes.

This other-thought, this "as-yet unnameable," is perhaps a promise, the sign of a happening in a world to be transformed. Doubtless, an endless task. However, in thought (let us call it thus), there are no miracles, only ruptures.

(1981)

II. On precolonial hierarchy

(reading protocol)

This reading protocol, although dated, is an application of this double critique. As it is, this application concerns solely the analysis of the discourses *on precolonial hierarchy, and therefore does not present a portrait, an analysis of these societies as we could have drawn ourselves.*

1. The Khaldunian system

What are the hierarchical orders of precolonial Moroccan (and Maghrebi) society? In this regard, can we speak of segmentary systems or of the Asiatic mode of production?

Before we point out the contribution of these two approaches (Marxist and anthropological) to the knowledge on this type of society, we should for a moment return to the inevitable Ibn Khaldun, because this thinker—extremely original in his time—constructed a theory of the social system that concerns our object of analysis directly—and because a certain actualization of his ideas lives on intensely in Arab consciousness and ideology. We could rightly ask whether this return to Ibn Khaldun is not transformed into a simple ritual and whether this rogue paternity claimed by Arab thinkers would not betray a theoretical deficiency. Would the parasitic discourses developed on Ibn Khaldun turn out to be only a savage affirmation of identity?

No doubt, history as praxis and knowledge cannot escape being the object of such fetishization in our countries. And what's more, we know that history cannot claim to be detached from ideology, nor can it claim to properly ground a formalized knowledge. At best, the historical method—principally praxeological—finally responds only to a certain interrogation on identity.

Either way, the Khaldunian system happens to be at the very heart of our debate. Precisely in that this thinker considers his fundamental project as a discourse on history—hence, we think, his actuality. And also in that the epistemological rupture introduced by Ibn Khaldun into Arab historiography coincides, in the fourteenth century, with the decline of a part of the Islamic Empire. Other ruptures (political, economic, and religious) accompany this crisis. Historians of the Arab and Muslim world unanimously assign this period a strategic position in the history of these countries. It therefore represents a decisive period. The Islamic Empire was moving into a state of crisis, while the West embarked on an imperial movement that has defined it to date. We know the processes of this decline. The Islamic Empire breaks apart in every sense by the autonomization of the states, the city-states, and the principalities; knowledge takes refuge in religious exegesis and the subtleties of an infinite discourse on the hidden Word of God. Being the disillusioned observer of this troubled period, Ibn Khaldun retreats from political affairs and, in great haste, undertakes to write his masterpiece.

a. Two readings

A first reading of *Prolegomena* would stick to responding to the explicit project of Ibn Khaldun, who intended to create a novel science and give it a status. A novel science, which he defines very clearly: "It is actually an independent science whose specific object is human civilization (*al-umran al-bachari*) and human society (*al-ijtima' al-insani*). It has its own problems as well, which it must resolve: those relating to the essential conditions of civilization—one after the other. The same is true for all sciences, whether it be based on tradition or on reason."[8]

Being aware of this originality, the author is careful to emphasize the autonomy of the novel science in relation to the other disciplines, and repudiates dynastic historiography, which he denounces for its methodological deficiency and its social function of mystification. If, in the great Abbasid and Umayyad epoch, historiography was a codified science capable of administering—in its own manner—the vast Muslim Empire, afterward it becomes a simple discipline of genealogical recording, in the service of the ruling class, whereas for the author, it is a question of understanding the foundation of this ruling class. Thus, breaking away from all domesticated history, he intends to promote a critical knowledge (of which he defines the principles), the theoretical field in which history should henceforth be practiced, on the basis of its own set of problems, and with the help of God. That this explicit project presents itself as an epistemological rupture, there is no question about it. "All that is intelligible and real, he writes, calls for a particular science."[9] He goes further, declaring that this rupture is not a chance occurrence, but itself a historical product and a warning of God, the two being linked together in the same Khaldunian dialectic. Reflecting on history in the aftermath of the Great Plague of 1348, Ibn Khaldun writes, "The face of the inhabited world changed ... As if the voice of the universe had called the world to forget and shrink; and the world answered the call ... When a general upheaval takes place, it is as if the whole creation has changed, as if the world has been transformed; one could say, a new creation, a new world. It is also necessary that today historians paint an overall picture of the countries and the peoples, the conventions and the new religious beliefs ... This should serve as a model for future historians."[10]

God has spoken, history has changed, and Ibn Khaldun will be the witness of this mutation, the one who knows how to hear in the "Voice of the Universe" the frailty of all knowledge, of all human discourse.[11] A new knowledge and a new discourse are then necessary, not in order to ground historicity (save that of a cyclical time), but in order to grasp the signs that make man tremble before the finitude of his knowledge.

A discourse on universal history:[12] this is the Khaldunian project. But what discourse? And here lies the relevance of the second reading, which would stick to extracting the signifying system in which the discourse, its polyphonic structure (voice of God, voice of man) is developed. We mentioned that Khaldunian *al-ijtihad* is itself conceived as maximum reason (science) in maximum theology.[13] To create historical knowledge is, as Nassif Nassar puts it very well, "to inscribe in being a reality threatened by nothingness."[14]

Furthermore, Khaldunian discourse is placed both outside and inside history. Inside, to the extent that it brings about an overthrowing of historical knowledge, and outside, to the extent that this project, by overflowing the classical episteme, founds a new science. Then how to name this science? Hence the temptation to tuck it very quickly under sociology, history, or what has been designated by *'ilm al-'umran* (science of civilization). Let us leave this process open, without naming the project, without enclosing it within a science that would be external to it. Let us rather try to decipher it in its own movement and understand how the hierarchical order is formed therein.

Ibn Khaldun's ambition was to construct, through the theory of cyclical time, a social system, as a whole signifying, highlighting the interdependence of social subsystems and the tension between the different aspects. In a word, he sought to be a dialectician. This originality has struck many researchers of our century and continues to fascinate. It is necessary, however, to put this originality into perspective.

By adopting a method of structural exposition, and by preceding every chapter with a theorem-title, the author introduces a method that breaks with the linear discourse of history and with genealogical and narrative historiography. This shattering of traditional historical time, this decentering performed within the space of the text, confers upon this work a certain intricacy, especially when Ibn Khaldun sometimes contradicts himself from one chapter to the next, which results in the evident conceptual instability. For example, we can count several definitions of *asabiyyah*, but obviously these are only pertinent in relation to their position in a regional structure of the text (a chapter, for instance). Researchers, instead of following the movement of this dialectic, have in general juxtaposed these definitions. Afterward, and step by step, it would involve going through the Khaldunian epistemological field, through progressive-regressive syntheses.

b. Dialectic and cyclical time

According to Ibn Khaldun, the first postulate for the intelligibility of every society is that "man is political (*madani*) by nature."[15] This is how the culture-nature relation is presented: God created the Universe according to his will; he changes it according to his will; what is cultural is natural; it is nature that disposes of the world, as mediation between God and his creatures. To separate the state of nature from the state of culture presupposes the shattering of the theocentric idea.[16]

Ibn Khaldun explains his postulate as follows: "Social life is therefore indispensable to humanity. Without it, men could not fully assume their existence, nor could they carry out the divine plan of populating the earth by themselves, as representatives of God. This is what constitutes civilization, the object of science before us."[17] Culture being the naturalization of man, "power (*mulk*) is a natural (*tabi'yya*) quality of man, which he cannot do without."[18] But if all that is cultural is natural, this does not mean that societies live in a world with no values. Ibn Khaldun is led to separate himself from other philosophers on the problem of prophecy, for instance, which, according to him, can be neither necessary nor natural. Prophecy belongs to the realm of the supernatural, and "logic has nothing to do with it."[19] That is why, in a theocentric culture—like Muslim culture—discourse is at once on man and on God. And it is by means of this three-coded grid (doxological, narrative, hermeneutical) that the signifying system of *Prolegomena* should be extracted.[20]

We know that the Khaldunian project itself develops and is developed in a theory of cyclical time, by means of which Ibn Khaldun returns to a fundamental, but still as powerful myth of humanity.[21] We say that mythical time and historical time intersect, but are not confused with each other. Let us add that they exist—to varying degrees—in the same consciousness, and in such an intimate manner that analysis remains blind to such a constitution.[22] Hence the ambivalence of the Khaldunian project and the extreme tension that characterizes it. It is within the sphere of this myth (cyclical time) that the thinker strives to construct what he thinks presents regularities, comparisons, and laws in societies, without however being confined to his theological universe. This cyclical theory is intelligible only as a degraded mode of history. Ibn Khaldun refers constantly to the initial model: the message of Muhammad. If history has left the land of Islam, what finality can be given to the latter, other than that of a degraded repetition? Unlike Nietzsche (the one of the Eternal Return) who calls man to overcome himself, Ibn Khaldun merely observes the degradation of man and clings on to the utopia of the origin and of the initial model.

This long detour is not useless, we believe, because it will help us understand better the apparent contradictions of our thinker. In fact, the *asabiyyah*[23] (socio-agnatic solidarity) that Ibn Khaldun makes the motor of history exists in its purity only in the most "feral" (in the sense of the closest to the state of nature) of tribal systems, the only one with a strong cohesion, a strict endogamy, an egalitarian balance, and a set of values based on military violence (courage, honor, refusal to submit). It is up to the tribes of camel-drivers to build (and to destroy), by these virtues, central authority, dynasties, kingdoms, and city-states.

And hence, historical time becomes a circle, which can only be opened by divine decision. Is this the end of history? In cyclical time, becoming is repetition, and it is based on the law of correspondence (similitude or analogy). Of these correspondences, the most important is the law concerning the destiny of dynasties: "As a general rule, he writes, there cannot be less than four (generations): the founder, his son, the custodian, and the destroyer."[24] This is the inexorable law of the relations Bedouin society/civilized society, city/country, State/society, and civilization/*ensauvagement* (in the above sense).

Let us consider the first relation: Bedouin society/civilized society. This relation is sustained by an economical and political interdependence. No doubt, the latter is superior to the former, yet for want of *asabiyyah*, the latter withers away, marching to its own death. By moving away from the state of nature, it henceforth reproduces itself in a vicious circle. *Asabiyyah* having weakened, religion thus becomes an institution among institutions, corruption reaches all the way to the mores, and military violence fizzles out. What then reigns is an impersonal State, separated from society and doomed to destruction. Hence the generalized critique of Ibn Khaldun, both against the tribal system and civilized society. Trapped in the circle of his cyclical thought, our disillusioned thinker remembers: he reminds Muslims of the foundation of the virtues of the initial model. But as this model is a divine and unique act, which repeats no more, becoming becomes unthinkable; it is a pure dissolution. One can easily see the fragile nature of the laws sustained by Ibn Khaldun.

Let us take a closer look at the elaboration of the Khaldunian system. There is no strict opposition between city and country. As a matter of fact, Ibn Khaldun distinguishes three groupings: pure nomads (the camel-drivers), sedentary nomads, and city-dwellers.[25] The first group lives in an extreme economic scarcity, confined to camel-herding activities. Ibn Khaldun includes therein the Arabs (Bedouins), Berber and Zenata tribes, and the Turks. But this extreme economic scarcity is accompanied by a strong *asabiyyah*, a very powerful system of self-defense. Then there is a homology between an extreme economic scarcity and a culture with strong values, the latter compensating for the former and balancing the social system of the camel-drivers. As such, this society has no historicity. It needs an ideology, a religion, which is alone capable of transforming this "feral" identity into a universal vocation.

As to the second group (sedentary nomads), it consists of sheep, cattle, and goat herders, and includes the Berbers, Turks, Turkmens, and Sclavons. Ibn Khaldun calls them Chaoui. Their economy is more diversified and plays a mediating role between the other two groups.

The third group (city-dwellers) originates from the two others. Ibn Khaldun analyzes the different levels of their interdependence, while stressing the domination of the country over the city. "If the Bedouins," he writes, "need cities for their bare necessities, the city-dwellers need the Bedouins for the superfluous. The Bedouins need the cities for what is strictly necessary, precisely because of the kind of life they lead, as long as they live in the desert and have no political authority over the cities. They must work hard, in their self-interest, and eventually obey the inhabitants of the city."[26] Domination of the city-dwellers over the Bedouins—yet civilization, in moving away from the state of nature, is a degradation of man. From then on, it encloses man in a vicious circle: *asabiyyah*, as we know, weakens; military violence gives way to passivity. The city-dweller submits to the laws, and religion becomes external to him: "Religious law has become a simple branch of knowledge and a technique acquired by instruction and education. People have become settled and taken on the character of abiding by the laws, which leads to a diminishing of their fortitude."[27]

So here we are in a stratified society, no longer defined by the elementary structures of the hierarchy such as the *asabiyyah*. Rather, what we have before us is a political society, in which religion itself becomes a simple institution of social mobility. We shall come back to the class system in Ibn Khaldun's work. For the moment, it is important to note that the hierarchical order he conceives of is based on the notion of "nobility," itself defined by a strong *asabiyyah* and an authentic genealogy. Yet "nobility" diminishes or disappears in the city-dweller— the latter often lives it only mythically, through the invention of a family tree, in order to justify the claim to power and to compensate for the degradation of mores.

Several consequences follow from this analysis. In the first place, the most "feral" nomadic society is an infra-historical society, but whose virtues are necessary for the foundation of a real political society. In the second place, this society has a relative marginality, since it can break out of its isolation, reverse the relation of domination, and conquer the cities and the central authority. Third, the relative autonomy of the tribal system thus depends on its capacity for self-defense and aggression on the one hand, and on the expansion of central authority, on the other.

Since this expansion is fluctuating, there is a vacuum between the central authority and the tribal system where it is precisely history that is at stake, depending upon the movement of cyclical time. One of the originalities of Ibn Khaldun is to have seen with clarity the importance of imperial geopolitics: there is no State without the domination of a vital space necessary for its functioning, but as this domination grows, it creates the conditions for its own destruction. This is how, by scattering itself throughout different strategic poles, or by shifting its center (the capital), the State tries to safeguard its vital space. The history of Morocco is a good example of this migration of the State.

However, the analysis of the disintegration of the State remains vague; here too we find the contradictions of Ibn Khaldun, who combines a dialectical method (whose object is geopolitical in this case) with his conception of cyclical time.

c. Hierarchical structure

We had said that *asabiyyah* is a driving force of history. It is necessary to consider it on two levels: in its literal definition, when *asabiyyah* takes effect in an endogamous lineage, a pure lineage, and an unbiased genealogy; and on a systematic level whereby Ibn Khaldun builds a reference model, "for," he writes, "lineage is an assumption, not a fact." He cites the example of the Idrisids who managed to found a dynasty in Morocco, without *asabiyyah*. Once again, the concept remains unstable, as does the Khaldunian system. But after all, and as Ibn Khaldun says it himself, knowledge is also an art, that is, a discourse that requires a plural reading.

What is this hierarchical order, whose epistemological field we have tried to identify? "Nobility," says Ibn Khaldun, "is the secret (*sirr*) of socio-agnatic solidarity."[28] Nobility justifies the hierarchy. A *bayt* is a base nobility, whose members have more or less strong blood ties, but which at any rate is the dominant group. By referring to a *hadith* of

Muhammad,[29] Ibn Khaldun shows how hierarchy is at once a natural fact and a religious value.

Besides the family or families with blood ties, a base nobility (*tabaqat al-ashraf*) includes other categories as well: clients (*walā'*), allies (the *hilf* system), and slaves. Therefore, it is a veritable small political unity. Let us note that the relations patron/client, patron/ally form a solidarity similar to a common ancestry.

More exactly, we can say that there is a *particular asabiyyah* defined by blood ties, and a *general asabiyyah*, which is a political alliance.

Furthermore, the tribe is conceived as "a supraclanic patriotism,"[30] characterized by the most powerful clan. Supraclanic patriotism stratifies the tribal system into three categories:

1. the *chuyūkh* and the Elders,
2. the military guards, consisting of young men for the defense of the tribe, and
3. finally, the *āmma* (common people).

What about the historical evolution of this supraclanic patriotism? Is it the fundamental form of all tribal systems? What exactly do the tribal chiefs and the Elders represent, within the *jmaʿa*? Who had the right to bear arms? How was power distributed? So many questions, which remain unanswered, despite the fact that Ibn Khaldun talks of power, and especially royal power, in great detail. By contrast, he gives only a brief analysis of the urban social classes.

Remaining true to his dialectical method, Ibn Khaldun characterizes one of the forms of power in the following way: "Monarchy is a relationship between two terms. Government becomes a reality, when there is a monarch reigning over his subjects and governing their affairs. The sultan is the one with subjects (*raʿāyā*), and subjects are the people with a sultan."[31] Ibn Khaldun never loses sight of the fact that power is not an end in itself, but a means to administer society in accordance with the divine plan, thus preparing men for their destiny in the hereafter.

Then if this administration must be rational and just, nonetheless it finds its legitimacy in the use of force (this conception is not to be confused with Weber's, despite the apparent closeness of their thought). "Every monarchical edifice must be based on two principles. The first is force and *'asabiyyah*, that is, the army. The second is money, which provides the pay of the troops and maintains the structure of the State."[32] Once the legitimacy of power is predicated on these two principles, power is hierarchized along two main axes:

1. a hierarchy based on relations of kinship or clientele;
2. an administrative hierarchy, which he describes carefully and which obeys a principle that is still valid in our view: "The one assisting the prince can do so in several ways: by the sword, by the pen, with counsel or with science."[33]

Let us now move on to the problem of the urban classes, whose structure, in Ibn Khaldun's view, is based on the concept of *jāh* (political influence). "The *jāh*," he writes, "is largely distributed between men divided at all levels. At the highest level, we find the influence of the sovereign, which nothing surpasses. At the lowest rank, there are those who have nothing to win, and nothing to lose. Between them, there are many classes. Such is the divine order, which regulates the existence of its creatures, takes care of their interests, and assures their duration."[34]

We know that every power is legitimized in coercion that is necessary at once to the interests of the community and "to the divine plan of conservation of the species."[35] Ibn Khaldun, always armed with a Quranic verse or a hadith, justifies the order of values that sustains the hierarchical order he describes, while allowing for a certain dose of injustice. It is true that he describes injustice, for instance, with regard to the exploitation of the farmer, but at the same time, he encourages the capitalist system. On the one hand, he calls for coercion based on force, and on the other, for a moral self-restraint. It is easy to see the contradictions involved in such a problematic: every system thus constructed can only reinforce institutional classification.

It is necessary to add a few comments on the social classes, and especially on the relationship between the political stance and the economic stance.[36]

Faithful to his theory of cyclical time, Ibn Khaldun describes with a modern accent how, in a first instance, the State institutes a certain economic balance. Taxation is at first bearable by the population; it consists of a number of legal taxes: land tax (*kharaj*), *zakat*, and *jizya*, paid by non-Muslims. There is regular development and the civilization thrives. However, in a second instance, balance starts to dilate. In order to gain legitimacy, develop its clientele, and strengthen its army, the State imposes other taxes, whose religious value has often been controversial. These new taxes create a gulf between State and society, discouraging commerce, as well as the arts and crafts. Decline is accelerated. And, as A. Belal writes, "What is remarkable in this (economic) analysis is the dynamics of the relationships Ibn Khaldun establishes between power, its financial needs that are themselves the result of determinate moments in its evolution and its behavior, and the consequences engendered by these facts in economic activity, followed by a 'boomerang' type effect toward the base, that is to say, toward the ruin of economic activities and the decline of the State."[37]

We must add, by pushing Khaldunian thought a little bit, that the author is perfectly aware of the importance of the division of labor, as the determining factor of class formation. He knows that "social surplus product" is essential to social mobility and economic growth. Yet all these Marxist ideas *avant la lettre* unfold in a specific epistemological field. Then let us not push further the comparison with Marx and continue reading the internal structure of *Prolegomena*.

While Ibn Khaldun talks of an economic foundation of the classes, he never gives into economic determinism. Capital and labor only interest him to the extent that they constitute political instruments manipulated by the State. Social mobility is a function of the clientele system:

Every class, he writes, in a city or in a civilized country, exercises power
over the lower classes. To compensate, all members of a lower class
seek support from their superiors, and those who obtain it exercise
in their turn, over their subordinates, an influence proportionate to
their newly acquired authority. This is how social status acts on people
to let them earn a living. Its influence depends on the social class and
the social situation. The higher it is, the more profit it produces—and
vice versa. A private individual, however rich he may be, really makes
a fortune only in relation to his work, his capital or his undertakings.
This is true for merchants, peasants, and artisans. If they have no
influence, they have nothing more than the product of their work, and
will become destitute almost without exception. Either way, they will
not get rich fast. They will barely manage to survive, struggling against
poverty.[38]

This picture of the social classes clearly suggests that it is the clientele
system and political influence that are the main strength of a class.
Deprived of this political support, the intermediate classes (merchants,
peasants, artisans) risk becoming proletarianized.

But Ibn Khaldun does more than analyze; he makes a judgment; he
takes a stand. He describes the exploitation of the peasant, at the same
time as he encourages capitalistic development. His hierarchical system
is met by egalitarian ideology. Is this not an ideology that exists in the
present Arab consciousness?

That is why we believe it is erroneous to compare Ibn Khaldun's
thought with that of Marx, even if they seem to meet on certain points.
Theocentric historicity and the idea of cyclical time are opposed to the
finality of history, in Marx's thought. Where Marx intends to abolish
capitalist hierarchical order by undermining the values on which
this order is based, Ibn Khaldun makes a critique while justifying the
hierarchy of Arab society and a certain aristocratic vision of the social
structure. While Marx anticipates the end of the exploitation of man
that is supposed to bring closure to the end of prehistory, Ibn Khaldun
refers to a cyclical finality. Ultimately, the disillusionment of the one
faces the militant optimism of the other.

d. *Reinterpretation of the Khaldunian system*

Yet Ibn Khaldun's work stands in stark contrast to the intellectual production of his time and remains unique in this period of decadence. A. Laroui has explained how Arab historiography is domesticated by separating itself from critical analysis and how it becomes a narrative discourse of legitimization of the ruling class: "The more the State comes apart," he writes, "the more historiography is localized: tribal chiefs, chiefs of *zawiyas*, and *sharifs* have their followers who describe their actions."[39]

And one can only agree with Laroui when he invites us to rethink Maghrebi history both outside the Khaldunian system and against colonial historiography. This double task is of epistemological importance: it is a question of decolonizing history, of returning the Khaldunian system to the classical Arab episteme, in order to analyze the latter as an historical product; this double task would allow us to identify more clearly the specific movement of the social structures of the Maghreb and their hierarchical articulations.

It is also true that the consideration of Khaldunian thought through colonial historiography[40] prompts us urgently to reactivate a theoretical reflection on the currently dominated societies, in relation to a thought of difference. By creating a dense ideological screen around its object of analysis, sustained by a discourse that is itself degraded, colonial historiography makes Maghrebi history illegible, except as that of a "colonizable"[41] society.

Let us now return to Ibn Khaldun and his system. In constructing a theory of the social system, Ibn Khaldun overestimated tribal force; he made it the motor of Muslim, and even universal history. He did not know that another model of society was taking shape in the West; he also did not know that other models had developed elsewhere, on other grounds, such as those "hydraulic societies" theorized by Karl August Wittfogel,[42] societies in which the tribal system is dominated by a centralized State, a strong bureaucracy that runs a government that is the biggest landowner and owns the principle means of production.

This is why *asabiyyah* as concept is at present unworkable and, as A. Laroui notes, it is "far more a secondary, induced phenomenon than a determining cause."[43] Generalizing his critique, the same author writes, "The tribal system, in all its aspects and with all its subsystems, must be described at the moment when it appears or reappears in history, after the Roman conquest, and not preconceived as a basic system at the very source of history. Its lasting importance in the Maghrebi past does not lie in the fact that it has conditioned an evolution or stagnation, but in that it was a dialectic response (whether new or revived is of secondary importance) to a blocked historical development. This accounts for its twofold aspect: on the one hand, permanent as a means of self-defense and guardian of tradition, and on the other hand, transitional."[44] In this passage, Laroui situates Khaldunian theory within history. Did Ibn Khaldun think that the Muslim world was no longer capable of building States? It seems so. In any event, starting from a disenchanted judgment on the period of decadence, on the crisis of the Islamic State and of its legitimacy, he was tempted to believe that the Islamic Empire had entered a cyclical time, that is, a degraded and repetitive form of a model forever lost— therefore utopian in a way, by the metaphysical closure to which he subjects history, a closure that confronts the void. And if a sense is to be made of the event, it is this process through which "the historian gathers signifiers rather than facts and relates them, which is to say, organizes them for the purposes of establishing a positive meaning and filling the void left by the purely serial."[45]

Do not these signifiers form an order of discourse that makes man tremble, beyond history, in a space (that of identity) where the sign, even protected by God, becomes unbearable to consciousness? Now that the Khaldunian problematic is consumed with the history of his time, we can resume the dialogue with Ibn Khaldun on another level. We have seen how, for instance, Laroui insists on the fact that the tribal system is an induced phenomenon, and not a determining cause. However, Laroui's critique, sliding along a properly ideological plane, is not exempt from ambiguity. By stripping historiography of its ideological weapon, he lets slip the dialectic of the trinary system of tribes/cities/Makhzen.[46] Ultimately, and as he strongly emphasizes in his conclusion, we arrive at a conception that overestimates, in reaction to tribalism, the role of the State.[47]

2. From Ibn Khaldun to Marx

This itinerary of the Khaldunian epistemological field is linked, however, to a double lacuna: we have neither a systematic study of Maghrebi historiography nor an economic and social history of the Maghreb at our disposal. But this double lacuna obviously should not prevent us from elaborating hypotheses on traditional hierarchies. The effort at theorization aims to address the anticolonial past with a more appropriate problematic and to ask historians the question of the very status of this economic and social history.

Three theories provide valuable contributions to the knowledge of traditional hierarchies: Arab historiography in its Khaldunian version, Marxism, and segmentarity theory to which we shall return below.

Therefore, three ways of looking at the social structure: in the first case, as a historical being (with cyclical time); in the second case, as a conflicting order between the different aspects; and in the third, as a logical game, manipulated—more or less consciously—by groups and individuals. These three theories, which claim to be resolutely objective, agree that every society develops a system of classification that tends to somewhat consolidate the social structure.

A certain continuity of thought might be envisaged between Ibn Khaldun and Marx, but it is a false transparency. Would it not be better to accentuate the difference which, pushed to its limits, would then make the desired continuity more visible and more real? For Marx— and this is a first limit—knew little of Islamic societies. His typology of modes of production does not make much reference to this civilization. Indeed, in his studies on India and China, Marx senses the specific presence of Islam and the social systems that presuppose it, but his thought remains closed to that world.

We must note, however, the unfinished study on Algeria, on which he worked at the end of his life.[48] This is an incomplete (consisting only of a few pages of notes) but remarkable study, where he concentrates on describing what he calls a "mode of tribal-communitarian land ownership."[49] He shows how the deterioration of tribal ownership due to the Turkish occupation weakened the tribal system, without creating feudalization in his opinion, because "the strong civilian and military concentration in Algeria ... excluded the possibility of the hereditary monopolization of local functions and of the transformation of their holders into large landowners, quasi-independent of the Deys."[50]

According to Marx, what we have here is an essentially patriarchal society, based on communal property, and precluding any possibility of feudalization. Marx knows full well that an appropriation by the State or by religious institutions has existed in precolonial Algeria, but what he points out is that there is no necessary and mechanical relation between feudalization and the deterioration of the tribal system—and that the French colonial rule was responsible for the acceleration of this deterioration with the mass introduction of private property. Speaking of property, Marx writes, "It was the general cry of the political economy of western Europe, but also of the so-called 'cultivated classes' of eastern Europe."[51] Ideologically, colonization fights against all communal property, because it is a "form that encourages communist tendencies in people's minds."[52] Marx does not fail to note this semantic slide, which justifies with some derision the colonial politics of expropriation. The *colonat* will therefore be the driving class, which will make Algeria pass from the deteriorated tribal system to a capitalist society. In this perspective, precolonial Algeria is a variant of the Asiatic mode of production. Neither Marx nor Engels had the opportunity to clarify this fundamental issue.[53]

a. *Maghrebi society and the Asiatic mode of production*

With the decolonization of the Maghreb, the discussion on the Asiatic mode of production (AMP) and that of precapitalist societies is resumed, especially since the significance of an unpublished text by Marx discovered in the sixties.[54] "The exceptional importance of the *Formen* and the fragments it gathers and elucidates," writes Maurice Godelier, "is due to the fact that, through their content and beyond the notion of Asiatic production, they compel us to pose again in a non-dogmatic manner the fundamental question of the conditions and forms of transition from classless societies to class societies, and of the differential and unequal evolution that results in the formation of contemporary societies."[55] We see here, in the words of Godelier, the same ambiguity that weighs upon the Marxist analysis of the hierarchies in non-European societies and the evolutionist tendency that marks the typology of the different modes of production.

In an interesting book, Yves Lacoste[56] has attempted to respond to this concern by an interpretation of the specific social structures of the Maghreb, drawing mainly on Ibn Khaldun's *Prolegomena*. Lacoste, moreover, broadens the discussion and compares his own analysis both with Marxism and with K. Wittfogel's theory of hydraulic societies. His response is at once hesitant and original. He says the Maghrebi society of the Middle Ages presents a certain similarity with AMP, since:

> The dominant mode of production in medieval Maghreb, as in most parts of the world, is essentially characterized by the following:
> 1. The insertion of a vast majority of the population into a group of autarchic or quasi-autarchic village or tribal communities;
> 2. The presence of a privileged minority whose members enjoy significant benefits but without a right to private property on the means of production. These are the two basic characteristics of what Marx called "Asiatic mode of production."[57]

While advising extreme caution with the use of AMP, Lacoste curiously speaks of an "artificial mode of production" in the sense that the fragility of medieval Maghrebi economy, which was essentially a market economy, did not culminate in the formation of a bourgeoisie that would have allowed Maghreb to move from a precapitalist structure to a capitalist one.

This comparison with the particular evolution of Western Europe ultimately eliminates one hypothesis, which, from the outset, was unworkable as such. Lacoste, dismissing Wittfogel's theory, characterizes medieval Maghrebi society in the following way: "This society is not only tribal; the role of the merchant and military aristocracy is essential therein. It is not a slave society either; there are many slaves, but they are not involved in production ... There is no seigneurial system and, for the most part, no private land ownership. In North Africa, there is neither a true nobility, nor professional warriors (aside from slaves), nor a true bourgeoisie."[58]

Lacoste, apart from these entirely negative definitions, paints a general picture of this variant of AMP. Medieval Maghrebi society is dominated by a market economy; the State and the mercantile aristocracy control the famous Gold Road. Suppose this first proposition is valid; it needs to be demonstrated that slavery was a minor phenomenon. We know that a "caste" system still exists in the south of Morocco. Even if Islam has integrated converted slaves, it should be recognized that this manpower was an economic force, and that it was itself a sort of means of production. We need economic anthropology at this stage. It means asking historians the question of the actual importance of these two phenomena (gold, slavery) and their impact on a composite economy, driven by different modes of production.

What then becomes of the hierarchical system in Lacoste's problematic? He identifies a general structure characterized by the following:

1. A relatively weak State, which relies mainly on taxes of gold and taxes allowed by Islam; this State does not appropriate the means of production, even if, says Lacoste, a certain appropriation of the land did exist, which will be the sign of a gradual feudalization.

2. A merchant aristocracy, playing the same role as the bourgeoisie in capitalist societies, but which is weak, despite the advantages granted to it by the State[59]: "North African aristocracy remains relatively unstable, and fails to attain a structure, or to maintain itself as a hereditary group."[60]

3. A tribal and military aristocracy, consisting of tribal chiefs and big families, who use blood ties and the clientele system for the manipulation of power; but the legitimacy of military violence is not guaranteed, since every man has the right to bear arms.
4. A community-tribal system, seemingly egalitarian, but actually dominated by the tribal or military aristocracy.

In short, Lacoste thinks, "in North Africa, there exists basically only a hierarchy in fact, and not by right, between tribes, and not between individuals."[61]

Lacoste's analysis—like many others—is confused in the face of the very flexible arrangement of the social structures in the Maghreb—an arrangement characterized by a process of open social mobility and the nonsolidification of a class structure. That is why, when he addresses class conflicts,[62] Lacoste renews the dualist illusion (between the tribes and the Makhzen). For it remains debatable whether the peasant revolts are conflicts between these two systems only (Makhzen and tribal); we think that a class divide comes in tandem with a tribal divide, and that a true class struggle breaks out between the Makhzen and the tribal aristocracy. The question is to determine in each case the driving groups, which derive from multiple hierarchies, and which guide the social movements.

This problem is taken up again in more detail by another Marxist at a conference on "feudalism." René Gallissot states in his remarks that "social struggle in the country is no less of a class struggle, although the generality of the expression 'social struggle' is more appropriate."[63] Gallissot, analyzing precolonial Algeria, places Marxist theory on a more subtle level than Lacoste. He denounces the myth of so-called Berber democracy, brought forward by colonial sociology and ideology in order to justify the French penetration in Maghreb. For this sociology, imperialism is legitimized simply because it restores to archaic democracy its right against the Arab feudal system. Gallissot understands the fact that the system of *liffs* (or *saffs*) is not the ground of a tribal legality, but one logical system among others, used by the Makhzen and the rural aristocracy to dominate the tribes.[64]

On the basis of an analysis of the different modes of appropriation of land (and of water) and of the means of production, Gallissot demonstrates their origins as such:

1. Collection of taxes and their harvest shares by the State (and by the classes related to it). So-called *habous* land created a seigneury whose political role is well known.
2. A certain concentration of private ownership and of the means of production due to the control of the economic "surplus" by the ruling classes.
3. The power of command is itself the decisive level for the control of scarcity.

Thus a class hierarchy is formed, based on four levels:

1. A communal peasantry whose economy is characterized by the combination of a tribal mode of production and a weak appropriation of the modes of production. The *khammas* paid in kind constitute an equally weak class. Gallissot believes that these are the essential traits of a precapitalist society.

   This is indeed an exploited peasantry, but without class-consciousness, whose revolts lead nowhere and fall into "superstitious or mystical loss."[65] But Gallissot leaves it at this far too general statement. In fact, what does a religious loss mean? Would the peasant revolts be due to a simple ideological illusion?
2. Above this peasantry is a rural aristocracy who owns lands and holds a political and religious power, and has complicated relationships with the (Turkish) Regency.
3. The urban mercantile bourgeoisie does indeed own a certain patrimony and certain means of production (trade, industry), but it is dependent upon the Regency; it is furthermore incapable of accumulating capital. "The control of goods," writes Gallissot, "is the promise of capitalism: the loss of commercial control condemns society to an increasingly rigid feudal structure, and to the decline of the return to the land."[66]

4. The State is formed by a command aristocracy (political and
   military), which controls the collection of taxes and the essential
   means of production. And Gallissot concludes, "It is through
   the rule of this public administrative military upper class that
   European feudalism eventually differentiates itself from the social
   structure of the Regency, and still only relatively."[67]

The reinterpretation of the notion of command aristocracy, studied
by R. Montagne, needs some clarifications. In a society—such as
precolonial Maghreb—where several kinds of the appropriation of
economic goods coexist, politico-military violence is as important as
the economic aspect. This is where Marxism falters.

By stripping tribes of their military violence, the State lays the
ground for an appropriation of space and economy. The control over
violence precedes or coexists with the manipulation of scarcity. It
is at the moment when tribal resistance at this stage of its history is
weakened that anthropology has a reason to exist: the kinship system,
the segmentary system are so many answers to a dispossession of tribal
authority by the State. Anthropology has to address this problem, or
else it risks considering (which happens often enough) the provisional
disempowerment of the tribal system as a genetic structure of every
tribal system. In other words, anthropology cannot do without a
historical discourse, which refers it back to its own ground.

The appropriation of the means of production by the State is
only the second stage of this dispossession. Marxism, by insisting
on the categories of capitalist economy (private property, means of
production), misses the progressive-regressive movement of the tribal
system. Marxism says that the tribal system could not reach its full
potential in the development of productive forces. Yet it is not that the
tribal system does not know how to accumulate goods; it institutes in
the economic game a surplus "for the functioning of social structures
(kinship, religion, etc.)."[68] Western bourgeoisie, while assuming the
industrial revolution, at the same time imposed a fierce rationality
(of productivity); it thus laid the foundations for the socialist utopia,

which would ensure for man a real appropriation of his historical being. Through this broadening of the concept of "productive forces," we may reconsider certain Marxist hypotheses, by comparing Marxist thought with economic anthropology. We should be grateful to Marcel Mauss who, in his admirable essay *Le Don*,[69] described how exchange maintains the balance between scarcity and the dangerous excesses of the inequality of social structures. But when the economic rationality of the tribal system was broken or weakened by capitalist economic rationality, the tribal system continued to function in a degraded, segmentary mode, in the state of a latent resistance. It is to the illusion of a system that has lost its military violence that analysis must be directed. And if there is any process of feudalization, it is merely an induced process: private property takes precedence over the manipulation of scarcity and violence, and economic surplus takes precedence over social surplus.

This is why the AMP does not seem to be an appropriate designation for our object of analysis.[70] The same applies to the concept of pre-feudalism. The typology of modes of production elaborated by Marx was a working tool that was adequate to the level of knowledge he had of non-European societies. This typological model will have to be reviewed and validated by a more differentiated analysis.

However, through this confrontation with Marxism, precolonial hierarchies may be better understood in a macro-historical perspective, and thereby we can identify the strategic poles in which the different aspects come together and class structures seek to solidify themselves.[71]

3. The segmentary system

Khaldunian discourse and Marxist discourse, while sensitive to macro-historical movements, have often neglected the analysis of the internal organization of tribes and, generally speaking, the description of what Roger Bastide calls "the elementary forms of stratification."[72] In both systems, it is difficult to discern the transition from these elementary forms to a structuration of class. The historical anthropology of Engels (in *The Origin of the Family, Private Property and the State*) is based on a rather limited knowledge of non-European cultures; therefore, the method, the Marxist typological essay on societies, must be verified, reinterpreted, and incorporated into a knowledge that takes account of the contributions made by the human sciences since this attempt by Engels.

Anthropology, which for a long time showed little interest in the transition from elementary forms of stratification to a class structure, is starting to address the problem raised by Engels,[73] but after having taken a long detour. Among the most fruitful research in this area, let us mention the one relating to the segmentary system, which was applied to the Maghreb, either in a secondary manner, by Durkheim, or in a privileged manner, by the English-speaking anthropologists E. Gellner and D. Hart, and J. Waterbury.

a. Durkheim and the segmentary system

Durkheim, in *The Division of Labour in Society*, where he qualifies Kabyle society as belonging to "segmental societies with a clan-base" (clans to be understood in the sense of patrilineages), writes the following: "We say of these societies that they are segmental, in order to indicate their formation by the repetition of like aggregates in them, analogous to the rings of an earthworm, and we say of this elementary aggregate that it is a clan, because this word well expresses its mixed nature, at once familial and political. It is a family in the sense that all the members who compose it are considered as kin of one another, and they are, in fact, for the most part consanguineous."[74] I would like to quote two more short texts by Durkheim, rarely mentioned and analyzed by Maghrebi researchers, and which should have drawn their attention so as to compare their analyses with Durkheimian theory.

Durkheim clearly sets forth the conditions for segmentarity: "For segmental organization to be possible, the segments must resemble one another; without that, they would not be united. And they must differ; without this, they would lose themselves in each other and be effaced."[75]

The segmentary system is then a sort of chess game, a structure in which different segments have the dual characteristics of being homogeneous and similar.

Evans-Pritchard,[76] systematizing this game, presents the following diagram:

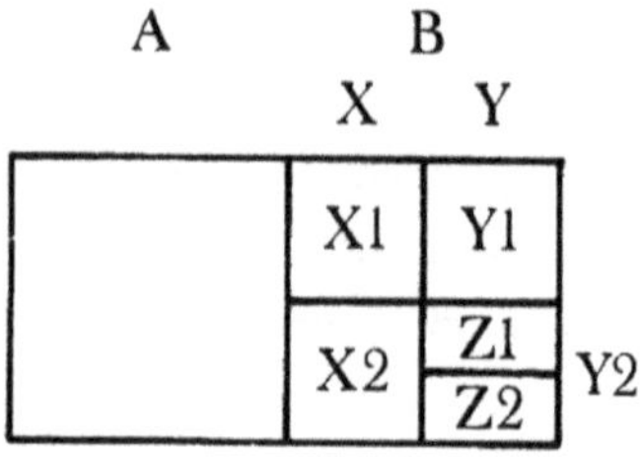

A	B	
	X	Y
	X1	Y1
	X2	Z1 / Z2	Y2

Diagram 1

When ZI opposes Z2, the game is played only between the two. But when Z1 opposes Y1, Z1 and Z2 conspire to form the same alliance Y2. Likewise, when Y1 opposes X1, Y1 and Y2 conspire, as well as X1 and X2. When X1 opposes A, the segments X1, X2, Y1, and Y2 conspire to become B so that balance is always restored.

In the same way, as we have seen, it is possible to produce two images that show the segmentary game in a patrilineal society. The first image represents the family tree as seen by the group:

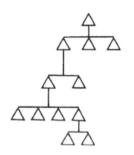

Diagram 2

This first image describes the mechanisms of fusion and fission (or process of union and process of opposition). The second image represents the position of the individual in a segmentary society, as set inside a set of concentric circles:

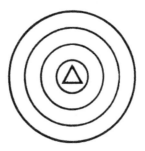

Diagram 3

The largest circle is that of the ultimate ancestor, but the more genealogical ideology moves away from individual memory, the more it tends to become mythical for the latter.

To return to Durkheim, the oppositions will be as follows:

- mechanical solidarity: segmentary organization, therefore decentered power;
- organic solidarity: state organization, presupposing the division of labor, specialization, and social differentiation.

In the segmentary system, cohesion is maintained by a prevalence of religion over power. If then this organization is egalitarian, the economic aspect is dominated by this game of chess, and Durkheim can write: "Communism, in effect, is the necessary product of this special cohesion which absorbs the individual in the group, the part in the whole. Property is definitive only of the extension of the person over things."[77] Durkheim thus joins Marx as they both ground social differentiation on the individualization of property.

In theory, the segmentary game, through fusion and fission, prevents hierarchization, and "in a segmentary system the position of an individual is defined neither by social stratification nor by a professional specialization, but rather by the totality of his vertical positions, each of which is completely impervious to its neighbors."[78]

Applying the segmentary system to Kabylie, Durkheim writes, "Thus among the Kabyle the political unit is the clan, fixed in the form of a village (*djemmaa* or *thaddart*); several *djemmaa* form a tribe (*arch*), and several tribes form the confederation (*thak'e-bilt*), the highest form of political society known to the Kabyles."[79] Yet Durkheim, relying on a second-hand source, is hoodwinked by the analysis of Hanoteau and Letourneux in what concerns the semantic confusions, the classification of different segments and their insertion into a more global context. And above all, Durkheimian theory liquidates history out of ignorance (?) of the specific evolution of the Maghreb, where centralized States have existed and were directly involved in the tribal organization. In that sense, the segmentary system is an epistemological illusion. Why? In addition to the reasons already outlined throughout this analysis, it is hard to see how the phenomena of fusion and fission do not entail the development of a condition of subordination/domination. Neither is it clear how this balance is maintained and how it escapes the history of global society. This methodological deviation has serious consequences. We uphold a different hypothesis, while taking into account the significant contribution of applied anthropology to the Maghreb.

It is also true that several anthropologists, in order to justify this logical game of segmentarity, rely on the discourse of self-interested society. There is a famous Bedouin proverb that says, "I against my brothers; I and my brothers against my cousins; I and my brothers and my cousins against the world." Without going into strictly linguistic discussions, this saying connotes something else; it literally says, "I and my brother against my paternal cousin; I and my paternal cousin against the stranger." The reinterpretation of this saying in the segmentary system, by a semantic slide, is untenable.

Having pointed out this detail, we come up against far greater obstacles. Indeed, a society is never completely segmentary;

segmentarists know this, and they say it. History shows us in the case of Morocco how a central force (the Makhzen for instance) disrupts the supposedly segmentary organization; the Makhzen, through military violence, makes a direct intervention, distributes the tribes, and relocates them. Likewise, an imbalance may arise at the very heart of a patrilineage, or of a tribe, for the appropriation of power. The Makhzen may also make alliances with the tribes. Finally, an important methodological remark fundamentally calls into question the application of the segmentary system to the Maghreb. When J. Favret[80] complains of the silence of the self-interested society, is she not aware that there exists a Maghrebi historiography and a tremendous stock of local archives? To reinterpret the Kabyle system on the basis of Hanoteau and Letourneux's work is to remain trapped in an ethnocentric hermeneutic circle, unless one wants to understand how the application of the Napoleonic code to the Kabyle society serves as a justification for a segmentary system whose theory is itself unreliable. The "sophistication" of anthropological theories, on the pretext of letting the object of analysis speak for itself, well conveys the great solitude of the observer, henceforth confined to the discourse of a lost identity. The logical systems of the anthropologists compensate for the derealized relation with their own history and with that of the societies observed. And hence, we think, the significance of this intellectual bricolage that builds, on the theme of difference, wild works of art based on a wild thinking. This is obviously a methodological delirium.

b. Moroccan society and Anglo-Saxon segmentarists

The same ambiguity affects E. Gellner's analysis of Moroccan society.[81] While Berque[82] calls into question the generality of the binary organization of the *liffs* previously described by R. Montagne, Gellner, as he criticizes Berque, thinks that binary organization is only one example of the chess game that segmentarity constitutes. And the example he gives is his analysis of Zaouiat Ahansal.

The following table represents the relation of power/society:[83]

	Marabouts	Berber tribes
Realm	Sacred	Profane
Characteristics	1. Pacific	Bellicose
	-neither war	-wars
	-nor dispute	-disputes
	2. Generous	Not necessarily generous
	3. Sharifian descent	Berbers
	4. Baraka	Lack of Baraka
	5. Orthodox Islamic faith	?
Political game	Neither violent nor fast	Fast and violent
Recruitment	Nonegalitarian	Egalitarian
	baraka/lack of baraka	
Election	Chosen by God for life	Elected by men for a year
Customs	Divine and intangible	Human and modifiable

Faithful to Durkheim and Evans-Pritchard, Gellner shows how this society functions through a decentering of power. This is a society of patrilineal filiation, of patrilocal residence, in which the grazing land and grazing rights are transmitted through the agnatic line. Moreover, two powers coexist: one is of religious essence; the *marabout* is chosen by the tribe and his power is permanent. And the other is of "secular" essence; the tribal chief is elected for a limited time, and there is rotation to prevent the concentration of power.

Generalizing the results of his study on Zaouiat Ahansal, Gellner eventually characterizes the tribal groupings in the Maghreb by their segmentarity and marginality. Logically, the two notions are complementary, but historically they express the same fact. Of course, Gellner knows full well that this marginality of the tribal system is relative, since it is social and not cultural: the Arabs and the Berbers belong to the Islamic community. Instead, emphasis must be placed on the idea of dissociation of the different aspects and of the predominance of one of them over the other, but at this point, further remarks on the segmentary system are necessary.

Theoretically, an atomization of the tribal system is impossible, nonviable; there is a level where hierarchy becomes necessary; and because of this necessity, it can and does provoke a stratification of roles and functions in the distribution of power. Sometimes it is segmentarity that overrides hierarchy and sometimes it is the other way around; what matters is to study the two systems in their historical unfolding. It is therefore possible to show that in the case of the *khams khmas* (five fifths), what we have is a balanced system allowing an egalitarian distribution of land and water (we know that the *khams khmas*, the *rba' rbo'* are Makhzenian constructions with fiscal objectives). However, between this and the transformation of this little system into a universal rule of the tribal groupings in the Maghreb, there is an abyss. The epistemological leap is not simple, and just as Alice can pass from the reflection of the mirror into the mirror itself, segmentarity jumps from one illusion to another. The tribe as genre is not static, and as the Moroccan sociologist P. Pascon[84] says, "The tribe at the time of the Saadi who attempt for the first time to set up a modern State, introduce slavery and try to establish a hydraulic society in the south of Morocco" is not the same tribe at the beginning of the Alawid era when "this dynasty struggles against local feudalities and tries to impose the Makhzenian model of Caidal society." The same author talks readily of the tribal system as not a marginal but dominated system. And we share the following critique of segmentarity: "Diffuse power, an equally-distributed burden, and rotation of sovereignty seem to be a fiction tacitly sustained by the chiefs of lineages during the early stages of the federation of lineages, but in fact every one of them knows full well where the reality of power is: it is in the number of men capable of bearing the arms that each lineage is able to gather together." Would segmentarism simply be the (ethnological) systematization of the dominating ideology of the tribal chiefs? It is a strange paradox that transforms an anthropological theory into a (unconscious) legitimization of the relation of domination! Theory of symbolic violence, which brings up again for us the problem of discourse: who speaks through the words of the anthropologist?

Our theoretical endeavor is moving in the direction of a sociohistorical perspective, joining that of P. Pascon,[85] who considers the tribe as "a political association based on economico-geographical factors: relations of man and soil, of human energy and the ecological wealth of a space at a given technological level."[86] From the association and dissociation of these lineages a movement of domination detaches itself, hidden behind the genealogical ideology of the supposed equality between the segments.

And Pascon concludes on the following point: "I would say that the modern North African tribe (nineteenth and twentieth centuries) is only segmentary provided that one forgets families and lineages exist at the bottom, and Makhzenian power exists at the top. It is segmentary neither in the micro-society nor in the macro-society. Segmentarity is in fact a form of flight from the imminence of the Caidal taking of power at an intermediary level between the lineage and the centralized State."[87]

The work of D. Hart likewise tries to apply segmentarity, particularly in the Rif.[88] He makes the organization into *khams khmas* (five fifths)— already noted by R. Montagne and Carleton Coon[89]—the key to Morocco's segmentary structure. This organization consists in a division of the tribe into five primary segments, which function according to the principles examined before. Hart notes three cases: the Aith Waryaghar of the central Rif (Abd Al-Krim's tribe), the Ait 'Atta of the central Atlas and the Jbil Saghru, and finally the sedentary Bedouins of Dukkala.[90] According to the author, this organization into five segments includes that of the *liffs*. The segmentary system is a "disequilibrium in equilibrium," and Hart accurately describes how it functions at the level of the different instances.

For the moment, we want to discuss two points: the institution of vendetta in this organization and the relative validity of this segmentary organization (*khams khmas*).

Several questions remain to be solved: what is the origin of this organization and how far did it extend? Is it due simply to an administrative division on the part of the Makhzen to collect taxes and a number of horsemen for its *harkas*? Or is it of a far more distant origin? And in that case, which historical function does it fulfill? It is now difficult to decide, because Moroccan historiography is yet to be carefully deciphered. But if we choose the first hypothesis (for a number of evidence works in its favor), it is necessary to show how this administrative organization is integrated into the tribal system, how the latter plays and manipulates it, in relation to the Makhzen. In any case, the question remains open.

The second point concerns the vendetta, whose function, as anthropology well knows, is to balance power by means of institutionalized violence. This is true when the segmentary system actually works, but an imbalance occurs (one patrilineage prevailing over the others), and the murderer is often forced to flee. This escape epically feeds oral literature and founds the narrative as the trial of a relentless military violence. The narrative is actually the degradation of myth,[91] but while the West would find a resolution to this trial in the novel, Moroccan oral literature—separate from written literature—is given over to mythical discourse.[92] This reflection on the folktale does not distance us from our object, for the tale is the formalization of social relationships in the order of discourse.

In any event, it seems that the Rif War, for instance, and the failure of the peasant revolt accelerated the process of emigration and allowed to find a solution to the tribal violence between patrilineages. Therefore, if the competition for economic scarcity and the appropriation of women necessitated vendetta, the tribal revolt against colonialism somewhat provisionally resolved tribal violence by means of a nationalist ideology, and economically by an increasingly massive emigration. Here again, the segmentary system is a fact induced by macro-historical events.

The same is true in the Rif for the institution of the abduction of young boys, which still existed in the nineteenth century. This institution used to safeguard competition for the appropriation of women in this patriarchal and puritan society. Now its function is changing: young boys, instead of being abducted, are made to dance in wedding parties. The boys, dressed as women, through this symbolic gesture, extend the homosexual violence previously resolved by abduction and rape. This is how prostitution thus allows the transition from a homosexuality connected to competition for the appropriation of women to a society where commercial sexuality once again saves puritan ideology. Just as the poor regions of Morocco provide the West with part of its subproletariat, rural commercial prostitution leads, at the end of each month (when Rabat's civil servants receive their salaries), to a migration flow and a fiscal levy.

Several consequences flow from this discussion of the segmentary system: in the first place, the segmentary model renders the processes of tribal stratification more intelligible, but it is useless when it comes to explain the place of the tribal system in history and in global society.

In the second place, this system does not account for the disequilibrium movements of the hierarchies between patrilineages, which constitute the many factors of feudalization and of the development of commanding classes. The transition from elementary forms of stratification to a class structuration does not interest the segmentarists, which limits the reach of their analyses.

In the third place, in a society such as Morocco, tribal organization is volatile. The intervention of the Makhzen, in different forms, draws a series of relations of domination and privilege in the tribal groupings.

In the fourth place, the demographic aspect essentially refers to an economic balance between segments and to a genealogical ideology; while the fission of segments is polyvalent, it might trigger emigration and a geographic mobility reacting to the allegedly segmentary system. Genealogical ideology is a derealized expression of the precise relations of force. In this sense as well, the segmentary system is an epistemological illusion.

When there is talk of a revival of this system[93] in present-day Morocco, what are we to understand by this? It is true that it is tempting to expand the notion of segmentarity to include the analysis of global society: segments thus become social classes, and the tribe, a class structure manipulated by the Makhzen. The status of the social classes would then be resolved by a sleight of hand. A regional theory cannot aspire to totalization in this way. Here again, anthropology (this time political) fetishizes an ideal type. But it can at least tell us how an epistemological illusion comes up against the concrete history of societies. It would be an unintentional contribution to the sociology of sociology.

4. Three models

Here then are three models, three discourses, which we have seen put to work on Maghrebi society, while pointing out the limitations of their investigation. We have insisted on the illusions that are likely to cloud our vision of the object of analysis.

All three approaches are meant to be resolutely scientific, each in its own way. They all make use of a type of logic: historical logic (Ibn Khaldun), dialectical logic (Marxism), and classificatory logic (segmentary system). But these three logics are deployed in specific discourses, each referring to a particular imbrication of codes.

Yet the theoretical differences between these models are to us more interesting. We have thought it useful to codify this difference in the following table:

	Khaldunian Model	Marxist Model	Segmentary Model
Actors	Tribes/ dynasties	Social classes	Patrilineages
Power*	Instability of legitimized violence	Appropriation of property and of means of production	Decentered
Time	Cyclical	Dialectical	Repetitive
Specificity of Maghrebi society	Dissociation of relation power/ religion	Pre-feudalism (variant of AMP)	Disequilibrium in equilibrium, or how to live in anarchy

*Power understood in the broad sense (political, economic, and cultural).

3

Disoriented Orientalism

We believe we choose freely to be what we are, but not being what we are, we are in fact constrained to play a role—and thus to play the role of what we are outside ourselves. We are never where we are, but always where we are only the actor of this other that we are.[1]

Pierre Klossowski

Exergue I

The act of bringing Orientalism back to its native soil without any attempt to tell of its cardinality (that has always oriented it) will always be somewhat contrived. There is always some artifice in supposedly making it shatter by brutally referring it back to the primacy of Western ideology and hegemony—a path that is limited in advance and reductive, but one we shall bring to light in this text.

Our question is about the East and the West in their essential spacing. It implicitly concerns being in its highest promise. And since every notion can be understood in a noble sense or in a base sense, Orientalism should be accorded its fullest desire for nobility, its nobility of view toward the sunrise. It is Louis Massignon who, more than any other Orientalist, honored this desire.

This nobility requires a delicate measure. It requires, vis-à-vis the other, knowledge of the laws of hospitality, a certain protocol wrapped in vigilance. Beyond all mutual resentment, it tells of the nuptial entry into the thought and memory of the other. Such a call puts one in a position to receive and go toward the other, to adjust language to the splendor of the Same. But perhaps we have forgotten the honor that we are owed. And perhaps our instinct of domination has drawn us away from such an encounter.

The Orientalist, noble in a sense, is the one who watches over the dawn of thought.

Argument

And where might this dawn be inscribed, if not in language? Language, inasmuch as it presents itself as the radical thought of a people. Dawn of thought here means the extraordinary synthesis of Being. This is the supreme idea the Arabs have of themselves. This willing thought that "honors the One" (Hegel)—what has become of it? For by insulting the nobility of radical Orientalism, Jacques Berque has reduced the East to a false story. We are responding to these murmurings and beyond, with a thrust that has become necessary, here and now.

In this book,[2] our author attempts to respond to the question of the Arab being through a progressive-regressive theme, frolicking between the present of the Arabs and their "fundamental" past; between the Quran and (pre-Islamic and modern) poetry; and between technology, decolonization, Egyptian song, the streets of Fez, and many other "incalculable" things. The book is an unsuspected treasure (oh how rich!), the only kind capable of explaining the Arab scene—a richness that is moreover adapted to its equally rich, equally perturbed field of analysis. "*Wijdan* (being) is, for the Arabs, a relation of essence to existence (and vice versa) that is particularly rich and perturbed."[3]

Everybody knows that J. Berque was a professor at the Collège de France. And clearly, this is not an accidental fact. Already at the beginning of this century, Le Chatelier was professor of Islamic sociology at the Collège de France. The same person created in Tangier in 1904 a scientific mission and in 1906 founded the *Revue du monde musulman*. "The object of this mission," later wrote Michaux-Bellaire, "was … to make, so to speak, a catalogue of Morocco, its cities, its brotherhoods; to trace its origins, its offshoots, its struggles and alliances; to track them in history throughout the different dynasties; to study its institutions and customs; to recognize in a word, as far as possible, the ground on which we may be called upon to operate some day, to enable us to act in full knowledge of cause."[4] This brief historical reminder does not directly mean that J. Berque is a legitimate heir of colonial ideology and of its Islamic sociology, under the auspices of the venerable Collège de France, the crucial axis of the exchanges between East and West. On the contrary, Berque is even a "theorist" of decolonization, far more fearsome than Frantz Fanon. In the insert of the book, it says that "it demands that the old Orientalism shatter itself." Let us follow the sparks of this shattering. Everybody knows then that Berque is a professional Orientalist who regularly publishes books on the Arabs ("his Arabs"). In the face of the complexity of the theoretical tasks that weigh upon the professors of the Collège, Berque gradually constructed a light regional "theory" on the Arabs and the Third World. This process of elaboration gathers momentum with the movement of decolonization. At first sight, this "theory" appears to be utterly capricious, eclectic, and straightforwardly opportunistic: it gathers elements and concepts drawn from different problematics. His books are wrapped up in an archaic and muffled language—a writing that cooks from below a fluid ceremony, a whole rhetoric of red herrings, slippages, toing and froings, and allusions; in short, we have here all the components of a semblance of thought, a theoretical artifice.

But such an artifice must be taken seriously: it conceals Arabs of a rare sort, and to whom we would like to pay a visit ourselves. Where do these Arabs come from? Where do they go? We might say that they come straight from metaphysics, in the Heideggerian sense of onto-theo-logy. Such is our hypothesis on Berque and on Orientalism as a whole—concerning the question of being. Metaphysics in its theological dimension, through the notions of the One and the Whole, founded that of God, that is to say, the notion of a prime mover and a prime being, which determines the hierarchy of the existents. That is why, when talking of Islam, the question of being is crucial, along with the whole ensuing chain of questions, the question of the One and the Whole, of the Identical, the Different and the Same, of Absence and Presence. The question is of such decisive importance that we can only indicate a direction here and point out the inner anguish of an affirmation. A polemical article is limited in its composition and strategy. It is written by an act of abduction, a detour of aggression. As an ironic shimmer on its own face, on the truth of its own mask, it tends to dialogue solely in the violence of interrogation.

As such, can Islam be easily circumvented by the metaphysics of Western origin? Where are we to place the intervention of Orientalism? It is now necessary to identify the dominant features of Orientalism, while trying to keep in sight the distant direction that underlies Orientalist discourse.

1. Inasmuch as it aims at the analysis of a determined (linguistic, historical, and religious) being called the East, without asking the question of Being and of the simulacrum according to a vigilant and rigorous thought of difference, Orientalism, in its stems, remains rooted in a metaphysical ground. As a matter of fact, it gives what it calls "the East" specific features, qualities, or virtues unthought-of in their irreducible difference. Arabism is thus characterized by a high spirituality and, simultaneously, by a fiery sensuality. And Islam is defined by a theological transcendence and a hypostatized history. In this regard, Massignon's dazzled work institutes a radical essentialism; Arab being is organized according to a threefold virtue: Abrahamic heritage, the given word, and the right of asylum. More than any other Orientalist, Massignon felt in himself the trembling of the question of Being. But this trembling remained a trembling, at the mercy of a mystical bend: for in making Al-Hallaj a Christ-like savior, he ended up Christianizing Islam. With him, we do not know what the specifically Islamic *ordeal* is, and how suffering is called as such by the Muslim.

Corbin's misinterpretation is even more notable. This Orientalist makes Heidegger's thought Shi'ite[5]; this thought, which, albeit mystical, actually claims to move toward the margin of metaphysics and of all theology.

The example of Massignon and Corbin calls for a detailed analysis. We are obliged to indicate a position here, an orientation, to the extent that the word "cardinal" remains caught by common language.

It is true that after the Second World War and with the expansion of the social sciences, Orientalism changed its methods and techniques of investigation. But the essential problematic has remained unchanged. Rationalist Orientalists are trying to analyze the economic and material structure of Arab societies. But as such, is not this rationalism of the social sciences a matter of the essence of technology and metaphysics, if we accept Heideggerian thought? By merely reversing spiritualism, Orientalism falls into an unthought-of materialistic field. The question of the East as such and as radical coordination to the West is yet again forgotten. Much could be said about the recent discussions between the Orientalists and Arab intellectuals, trying to find out whether the Arabs are overdetermined by the primacy of ideology or of socioeconomic production or of political practice. This slight shift of the discussion in no way implies a certain exit from metaphysics. At best, we are dealing with a generalized historicism, which demands that the West displace its ethnocentrism.

But as for J. Berque, it must be noted that he carries out an alchemical synthesis of all the points of view, according to an entirely ludic impetus.

2. The second dominant feature of Orientalism consists in its positivism that is not in contradiction with its spiritualism. We can therefore say that there is a coherent unity between essentialism, positivism, and metaphysics. Heidegger has posed the question admirably in his different meditations on technology. If we agree with him that the destiny of technology is the destiny of metaphysics, and that science presents itself as the supreme simulacrum (will of the will) of Western domination, we could perhaps better understand the position of Orientalism in the field of the social sciences. After being marked by philology, historiography, and culturalism, French Orientalism has lately opened itself to structural analysis, semiology, and Marxism. However, these knowledges are put on trial with regard to the question of their metaphysical basis. As long as Orientalism remains content to follow the dominant ideology of its time without trying to think it, as long as it does not reflect on its necessary margin, it will drag behind metaphysics. Just as a thought of difference begins

to impose a productive rigor, Orientalism pursues its positivist approach, as if Nietzsche, Freud, and Heidegger had never existed, and as if the thought of Blanchot and the vigilant thought of Derrida had never spoken, each in their own way, of the question of every West, and of likewise East. What is the use of attempting a semiology of the Quran (as Berque has done) if the East remains a false story, a mere humanist exercise? But we shall see that J. Berque's writing is marked by preterition (a word he especially savors). Preterition, according to le Robert, can be "the omission in the testator's will of a compulsory heir." Then, let us not forget the destiny of Orientalism in the metaphysical testament. But who will write this testament?

3. Orientalism, whether it is Christian, idealist, or rationalist, is in solidarity with humanism. Moreover, theological humanism finds a fallback shelter therein. When in the nineteenth century the scholastic God withdraws from the Western scene, leaving its place to man as the subject of history, Orientalism recovers it from the Arabs. By what inner necessity is Orientalism drawn to Islam? Is it because God has abandoned the West to a technical devilry?

In Massignon's vibrant eschatology, it is Islam that, at a moment of history, saves humanity (Abrahamic, of course). Islam would then reinstate faith. Christianity, which has deviated from its inaugural truth, according to Massignon, has forgotten its prophetic mission by covering over the colonialist crime, thereby violating the divine right of asylum on this earth. Likewise, Judaism has been lost in Zionism. Massignon's Abrahamic Allah maintains the word of the humble and the dominated, and prepares the grand reconciliation of the three religions.

Taking another path, Berque lays claim to the philosophy of Enlightenment, Rousseau's in particular. His references to Marx, Sartre, and Heraclitus ("the friend of things and our common father," he says) are therefore entirely superficial and circumstantial. He claims Rousseau as his spiritual father, like Lévi-Strauss who founded structural anthropology upon the theological nostalgia for the origin. The example of this humanism was admirably analyzed by Jacques

Derrida whom we continue to hold apart, because of his irrepressible passion for listening and for the gap, the margin that watches over its own simulacra. Derrida's thought is a leap toward a thought of intractable difference; have we fully understood this?

In any event, Berque's humanism, in all its aspects, calls for a teleology and a secularized eschatology, disguised under the name of "utopia." He wants "a system of the Earth."[6] "How to operate the encounter, he asks, with a project that is scientifically based on desire?"[7] This "operation" is already posed in the question of technology and its devilry.

In order to get a sense of the extent of the Orientalist fantasy, one should read the peculiar text of the debate between Berque and Massignon published in the journal *Esprit*.[8] It is true that the involvement of Jean-Marie Domenach (director of the journal) blurs the issue. For instance, he wonders if the Arabs are really capable of industrialization or of producing thoughts like those of E. Mounier and Teilhard de Chardin. He, moreover, ends up revealing his spiritual audacity: "But," he exclaims, "don't you think it is troubling that all these questions that arise on the Arab world are asked by us, and not by the Arabs themselves?"[9] As for me, I do not find it troubling at all because the questions you ask, Mr. Domenach, tell only of your prejudices— reread yourself word for word. As for Mounier or Teilhard,[10] let us be serious. Let us save the Arab world the trouble of dealing with them, and move on.

Berque's paternalistic and stilted rhetoric insists on what he calls the tension between the sacral and the historical: does he know of a society or a historical period where this tension is not at work? It is the characteristic of Being (in the Heideggerian sense) to happen in a correspondence between gods, men, and things. Of course, this correspondence may more or less occur in speech, but the fundamental question remains the same. Thus, the debate is in itself sterile when Berque calls the Arabs to protect their identity by appropriating technology: "What we can do is, beyond technology, reinstate values— but through and by technology; and I think, instinctively or consciously, that this is what the Arabs, like us, aspire to do."[11] This beyond (see below) is precisely unnameable. Technology is not simply a crossing for humanism—it bears the destiny of metaphysics.

On the opposite of this stilted rhetoric lies the generous eschatology of Massignon. As usual, he does as he pleases. He talks of the laws of hospitality, of the right of asylum, and of prison "which educates in freedom and (that) it is by this means that the Arabs will arrive at its fullness."[12] This debate took place during the Algerian war. Thus, for Massignon, the humiliation of the oppressed and the tortured would save Abrahamism and the meaning of the Christic ordeal. And as the debate came to an end, Massignon found a solution. Read carefully this duo:

> BERQUE: And this is why there is basically very little difference
>   between your positions and mine . . .
> MASSIGNON:—We are both from the Collège de France, and
>   that's enough.[13]

We told this anecdote only to show better how far the chatter of humanist Orientalism can go.

Let us resume.

True to the opposition between science and metaphysics of which he thinks he is free, Berque lays claim to the social sciences. He applies this opposition to Islam, without troubling himself over the fate of such an opposition in Islam itself. How did Islam receive this distinction? How did it construe, in its own language, Greek ontology? Until such interrogations are called for, the question of the Arabs will remain astray. So where does this Berquian scene take us? Orientalism takes place between two movements of metaphysics: the one of the Western tradition and the one of Islam—Islam, as gathered in the heart of the Arabic language. Berque carries out a double gesture in his text. On the one hand, he performs empirical fireworks on the Arabs and Islam—an empiricism that is transformed in many places into a lousy folklority, like the following flamboyant metaphor: "From the minarets, during the legal hours, echo the muezzin's cry in arabesque."[14] On the other hand, a spiritualist essentialism impregnates his entire work with a particularly Christian climate (oh, but of course, a secularized Christianity)—a climate where the Orientalist holds the role of an oracle, a paternal Messiah who shows the Arabs the path "to a new type of authenticity."[15]

"Be yourself," advises Berque to the Arabs, to "his" Arabs. But from what place does he himself speak? To whom does he speak, dead and living? Which Arabs did he fabricate for the pleasure of the eye? If the destiny of the Orientalist is to be a privileged smuggler between the shores of linguistics and those of ideas, if his destiny is an auroral calling, what bright future does Berque's work hold out for us? Let us follow him in this debate; let us follow this undertaking that is meant to be flowing, elegant, and "up to the minute." Let us follow this academic tradition in its exotic frolicking. Perhaps we shall be caught by surprise and shall have to face our bizarre effrontery.

Considered from this double viewpoint (polemical and onto-theo-logical), Orientalism conceals the laws of its composition through a dual transfer of its metaphysical ground. Whether it likes it or not, it will belong to an irreducible ethnocentrist tradition as long as the knowledge sustaining it is inscribed in the field of metaphysics. But on the other hand, Islam does not facilitate the work of the Orientalist. By a mirror effect, it lends itself to an already-made reading, following another path. A certain God of Aristotle entered Islam before the arrival of the latter. There remains the question of knowing whether Abrahamic theology (whatever its variants) is not based on a simulacrum of the Greek divine. Either way, Orientalism is condemned to invest the other by a detour of origin, and to send it off—when it gets in the way—to culturalism and historicism. In 1957, Berque writes, "The French language, I dare say today, remains the Hellenism of the Arab peoples."[16] What is there to say?

To simulate is to do like; it is to produce a simulacrum. In a strong sense of the term, "the simulacrum is not a degraded copy. It harbors a positive power which denies the original and the copy, the model and the reproduction."[17] Simulacrum is therefore a fiction necessary to the real for it to come back to itself, but transfigured into a rigorous illusion. This extraordinary operation is proper to art. But all simulacra do not have the same intensity. In the case of Berque, it is a minor art of hiding the Arabs. He wants to conquer the Arabs without founding himself under the sign of the Father and his own genealogy, by trafficking the metaphysical word, which takes hold of our author from all sides.

Historically, the word "Orientalist" dates back to the end of the eighteenth century. However, the first chairs in Oriental languages have existed since 1245, following the decision of the Council of Vienne.[18] This word designates a university specialization directed especially to the past of the East, its languages and its religions. As a whole, Orientalism is marked by two stages: the first extends from the thirteenth century to the Second World War. This Orientalism is driven mainly by history, philology, and ethnology. During the second period, which has barely begun, Orientalism is integrated into the field of the "social sciences"—with a particular gaze. Berque, "this friend of the Arab culture,"[19] lived this transition trying to theorize it in his own way. What does this transition say? Let us go back. Born in Algeria in 1910, Berque was the son of a colonialist in this country. Augustin Berque is also known for the finesse of a few rare articles. Besides, father and son have more or less the same style. Jacques Berque's research focused particularly on the social history of the rural world. With the engineer Coulon, he takes part in an attempt at peasant reform called "Sectors of Peasant Modernization" (SMP). The general residence in Morocco had agreed on a politics of increase in production, thinking they were facing the consequences of the war, the drought of 1945, and the demographic upsurge in the Moroccan population. This politics was accompanied by an attempt at giving this reform a "social and educational character" in order to break the bottlenecks due, it seems, to the archaic techniques and the stagnation of traditional society. Berque summarizes this attempt by a striking formula: "the *jemaa* is on the tractor."[20] He will later write—seventeen years after the start of this experience—"the Moroccan peasant movement ... is born from the meeting between a sociological observation—of the vitality of rural communities in the Maghreb—and a gamble on agricultural mechanization."[21] Gamble on what really? The answer is: on the maintenance of colonization. How to understand otherwise the following declaration by Berque himself concerning the supposed experience: "The problem, he writes, comes down to this: to combine and to meld into a single movement the rise of the indigenous and the entrenchment of the French."[22] Berque is a civil administrator. His stay near Marrakesh was recorded in his doctoral thesis. Since his settling in Paris, he outgrew the all too narrow framework of Morocco and became the Arabist theoretician of decolonization. It is this transition that Berque attempted to theorize. Only, when it is not thought as such, a historical transition is always a lapse. Berque may tell us that he shatters Orientalism, he may warn us that such a participating survey is meant to let beings and things come to it; with him, we are certain that we will go nowhere. Why so? This synthetic heir of Orientalism in the Maghreb experiences his era and his field of analysis ("his Arabs") like a little gobbling machine. See it for yourselves in the book, if you are curious enough to read it. From a social historian, he goes on to become a semiologist of the Arabs, skipping from one "theoretical" status to another without taking the time to breathe; so, here he is a semiologist after having been a pulsatile phenomenologist, inspired by a fallacious reading of Sartre (whose misadventures with Hegel's thought are furthermore well-known), having been (yet again) a Lévi-Straussian ethnologist, a structural linguist, and a psychoanalyst of dispossession and of the trance of colored and enthusiastic independences. Under the name of psychoanalysis, Berque aims at the unfathomable psychology of the depths that is based, as we have shown many times, on an "in-depth" theological representation. It is easy to identify in Berque's works the stages of this theoretical skipping. We prefer to avoid some of the details to follow this shaky whole. Besides, this theoretical rapidity and this dexterity, which is never destabilized by any new theoretical trend, have eventually baffled certain Arab intellectuals. The defeat is in fact complete when our Orientalist brings out, by giving it a little nudge, the artifice of the paradox: "If these (Arab) societies do not yet have the history they deserve, the Arabic language does not yet have, not even slightly, the societies it deserves."[23] Berque's "Arabs" dwell outside their language, outside language. Then where do they dwell? Perhaps Berque is implying something even more terrible: in order to be truly Arab, one needs to mutate just like in science fiction. But let us return to his paradoxical words. We would readily accept this proposition if it means the following statement: As such, Being is a loss of identity—that is, in a nutshell, the determination of the radical simulacrum, simulacrum par excellence. But Berque does not worry about metaphysics. He is a social historian, a sociologist who loves the Arabs ... for their savor. Yet another mystery to solve further below.

But let us look closely at how the Arabs roam in the dispossession of their identity and how they confront decolonization and technical domination. But also let us see how the Arabs write poems, play the lute, and tell stories. In short, let us see how they present themselves to us, these Arabs of Berque's. And "Harems, dare I say it, in the second degree."[24] We must insist on an epistemological issue, due, it seems, to the suave atmosphere of the Arab world: Berque lets the fragrances of Arabia come to him. And as a matter of fact (again, see for yourselves in the text, text after text), Berque has invented in the social sciences the technique of suggestion and of catchy paradox. He is a sensualist soothsayer who, every now and then, tosses a mystery at us, then moves on to something else, to another even more mysterious mystery. No wonder "his Arabs" end up living in clandestinity!

Let us recall the first lines of his *Langages arabes du présent*, taken laterally here. These lines pose straightaway the fundamental issue: "Why the Arabs?" he asks. Yes, why the Arabs, and not nothing? We are summoned to follow him in his questioning. Let us hear the direct question, in the form of an elegiac duo:

So do tell. But why the Arabs?
   – Without doubt, other domains of the planet, other histories of
man allow for these formulations and these hopes, but they do this

through specificities that are for me (and for them) full of different savors.

– Savor? I thought you were a sociologist.[25]

There is still time to allow him to speak: "Now, I would say, Islam is not so much the presence of the sacred in conducts, beings, and even in things, but their exposure to a totality of oneself, it being not only 'sweet' as Hegel would say, but intense, combative, and indeed virile. Arab Islam is warm totality."[26] Yet how does this promise, which is to say, this full, virile, warm, and suave atmosphere, speak?

Once more, who are Berque's Arabs? In what terms does he formulate the question? Let us hear him once more: "The contribution of their contemporary history to the theory and practice of civilizations is due to what this history has in common with all the others, or even more to what distinguishes it from them."[27] This is a false alternative insofar as Being, the Identical, and the Different tell of the Same and its simulacrum. What is always important is not identity in itself and difference in itself, but the relationship that speaks from one to the other. What distinguishes a culture or a history, or what distinguishes Being, is precisely this original gap that, in order to be heard, necessitates respect for the irreducible. According to this exigency, the other cannot be reduced or brought back to an essence, even if it be heavenly, warm, and fragrant. The simulacrum, which makes the ego an other of the other, is proper to thought and art. All of this, very briefly mentioned here, has become commonplace in contemporary Western philosophy. Then where does Berque live? Does he too dwell outside his own language? But we are so insensitive to this exile in Collège de France that we are called to ask the same question: why the Arabs, and not nothing?

After his *Les Arabes d'hier à demain* (1960), Berque continues to redefine the Arabs, but these redefinitions are sustained by a surprising metaphysical fidelity. Here are the most essential points.

What "characterizes" the Arabs is first their classicism and a remarkable continuity of identity. They are classic, to the extent that

Orientalist humanism finds in them a fidelity, a closeness to their past, and an impetus toward the origins. Berque tries to determine this impetus and this fidelity by many different notions dominated by the word *asala*, which he moreover translates incorrectly as "authenticity." What we prefer is precisely a more originary translation, as "originarity." *Asala* refers to the source and the origin in the scansion and the beating of the Same (and not of the Identical as Berque repeatedly says), on the understanding that the Same is what comes to pass as the irrepressible gap that ties difference to identity in itself. That is why Berque—the institutional Orientalist who officially studies the identity of the Arabs—misses the thought of difference, without warning, while claiming for them "the right to difference." This lapse ruins his entire endeavor. This can easily be seen in the use of the notions he savors: identity/difference, unitary/plural, specificity, *asala*, authenticity, roots, foundations, rerooting, dispossession, alienation … A whole set of dilapidated notions, leaning on the shaky Arabs … For since the Pre-Socratics with whom Berque curiously identifies in his wild moments, from the very start, the thought of Being has known how to distinguish the Same from the Identical. It has always sung the praises of this original gap, which is the reason why I am the other of the other and yet myself; since the dawn of poetry and myth, it has sung the intoxication of intractable difference.

As long as metaphysics is still a thought of being and nonbeing, of the one and the multiple, Orientalism is called upon to shed light on its own tradition, and to talk on the basis of it. The day (and what a day!) a thought of difference takes over from metaphysics, Orientalism will be able to free itself from itself. But in the meantime, we can mute Berque's propositions, which can be as ridiculous as the following: "What is unitary in the Arab world, and what is multiple? This is an issue which should concern, for instance, the directorate of Education and Culture, founded recently within the secretariat of the Arab League."[28]

Another Berquian characteristic of the Arabs is the supremacy of the sacred. The present destiny of the Arabs would be, as we have seen, a tension between the sacral and the historical, a tension of transition from one to the other. This is no doubt a common proposition in Orientalist ideology, but Berque's intervention is more precise and more attentive when he insists on what remains folded in Islam: paganism and naturalism, notably. He also celebrates, with a convincing tone, pre-Islamic poetry and its strange lyrical density. This poetry of the desert still remains a challenge to orthodox Islam. We shall come back to this celebration.

What does Berque say of the sacral? Since it is not thought as such, in its correspondence between gods, men, and things, the sacral is reduced to a "level" of Being. Berque turns this level into an empirical manifestation disseminated in language, ritual practices, and collective behaviors—a theological reduction of Islam. If it is an essential abode of the gods in the heavens and the heart of men, the sacral is neither given necessarily to a religion nor acquired by mere sincere belief. The emergence and the disappearance of this abode are a mystical—radically mystical—ordeal. What is more, this is the mortifying experience of the Muslim mystical poets. That is why, in this respect, we are surprised by Berque's silence on the mystics, since he readily talks about the ludic sacral. Is he not attentive to the song of Being, to this dionysiac divine call received by mystical poetry with such supreme subtlety? What orthodox Islam represses is not simply naturalism and paganism, but also mystical thought that, while working on tradition, subverts theology and decenters it. And as Jean Genet suggests, the Beloved of the mystics must be understood in its concrete sense for the wonderful thrill of great Islamic poetry—irreducible to any theological reading— to reveal itself to us. The mystic is not a mere "level" between *al-adab* and science, the religious sciences, philosophy, and metaphysics; it is the decisive question of the sacral and the divine abode in the heart of men. It is the strengthening of dionysiac being, the tragic simulacrum of metaphysics.

Does Orientalism put the common destiny of the Arabs and the West at stake? Has Berque renewed the question? Already one can imagine that such a crucial question is problematic for an Orientalist turned toward a single aspect of Being. What happens to such a destiny? Either the Orientalist places the East in opposition to the West on the basis of an essentialist division or he makes the Arabs into a variant of the West to the point where we are forced to ask Berque "why the Arabs, and not nothing?"

In this framework as well, the most adequate affirmation of the oppressed people is to decenter all totality, all globality, and to resist all universal devilry with a necessary thought of difference. This thought is their destiny; who will think in their stead?—Certainly not the Orientalist accustomed to making false syntheses of the one and the multiple, of the unitary and the plural. Moreover, for now, there is nothing to deny the structural solidarity between Orientalist ideology and the imperial form of the West; nothing tells us that Absolute Knowledge has ceased to inhabit Western thought in its most vigilant thought.

Since his book entitled *Dépossession du monde* (1964), Berque has insisted by preterition on his cherished theme—for the Arabs, how to protect their identity while industrializing the societies? Berque reasons in levels. The totality he imagines is the "warm" synthesis (effervescent, as poor Gurvitch would have said) between these different levels. Now the rhetoric of this crossover is itself moot when it engages in an atomistic licentiousness, walled up in the empirical closure. Heidegger splendidly kept in sight technology in its essence. Technology is not one level among others. It is not only the expansion of industry and scientific models, and it does not only ensure the globalization of consumption. Technology as such ensures the metaphysical destiny of the West. There is no safe place from where it can be mastered. As such, it harbors an unprecedented risk of Being. That is why there is no such thing as identity of Arab being on the one side and a relative shelter for technology on the other. What is the place of the scission of historical being? Alienation (in the Marxist sense) expresses the absolute devilry of man, inasmuch as the exploitation and the hierarchical aggression of classes make this man alien to his own face, to his own proximity. Strictly speaking, alienation makes him unrecognizable and thereby dangerous for the dominator. And, in fact, this unfamiliarity of the face of the other is realized by Berque unwittingly: "Yet, for the Arabs, for instance, to remain themselves while gaining access to the industrial world, which besieges them from without and invests them from within, they would need to impart to all the other modes the same as what they impart to their material advancement. It would be necessary for the culture of Al-Azhar to project itself in doctrinal elucidation and social ethics at the pace of the movement of industrialization in Egypt."[29] This perfect theological junction requires no strong comment.

The Orientalist is a translator, inasmuch as he enables passing from one linguistic shore to another. His dream is to be bilingual. How to go toward the language of the other and receive him in his own language? We are talking about the Orientalist who is attentive to the destiny of the West, and for whom Arabs represent a form of Western classicism. The destiny of the Arabs is then a metaphysical stage of the West. Berque "orients himself" on the basis of this second position. No doubt he repeatedly stresses the particular originality of Islam and the Arabs, no doubt he also insists on this relationship that makes the Arabs so close and yet so far from Europe. These are statements of principle, a little late in Berque's case, but no matter! For Berque, the destiny of the Arabs is to be surprised by history and to arrive on a global scene occupied by industrial civilization. What does the historical retreat of the Arabs during the centuries of "decadence" say in itself? Since when does the retreat of Being stand for a delay? And with respect to what? But Berque forges ahead. He likes to dream about a globality, "a system of the Earth" that would save the plurality of cultures and societies. He dreams about a dialectic of "the unitary and the plural"; he calls for an absolute decolonization on the understanding that this means "to renature culture, and to reculture nature: and this is the true meaning of decolonization, and indeed of all revolution."[30] Only, what does globality mean as such? Does he (this secondhand utopian) believe that the logic of technology and its will to power are so controllable? What we make out is rather the signs of a tremendous enslavement of peoples, whether industrialized or not—enslavement that is not understood on the basis of an eschatological representation, but as a will to power devastating itself in its own being. At any rate, we do not want to preach any finality or make a Fanonian call. At any rate, we need to march on, and march on endlessly. And in this march, we are tied to the bilingual dream. But the essence of poetry is to be untranslatable. How to approach and listen to this untranslatable? The German Herder was asking himself in the eighteenth century, "Where is the translator who is a philosopher, poet, and philologist all at the same time? He should be the morning star of a new era in our literature!"[31] In other words, one has to be Nietzsche to be a translator, which is to say that translation is such an exceptional bliss that it comes only once in a while in the destiny of humanity. Does one have to be a poet and a philosopher if one is radically Orientalist? Without doubt, yes, when one does not separate thought from the language that shelters it, or the signifier from the signified, or form from matter; without doubt, yes, when one makes one's way toward a thought of difference. Only *the text* can give words to difference. Why? A language that transports another must be transformed during this journey while remaining itself—a rather strange and formidable transformation when the two languages belong to different linguistic sources and to two different metaphysical movements. Such that to be rendered in a legible transportation, this strangeness must obey a dual thought of difference, a radical gap. Without this radicality, the transposition remains transposition, the other remains an other without coming to pass in me as a rerooting, an *ensourcement* of my being. In the notes to his *West-East Divan*, Goethe makes a distinction between three types of translation: a translation that "acquaints us with the foreign in our own sense," a parodistic translation that "seeks to appropriate only the foreign mind, but by adapting it to our own," and a third that "aims at identifying itself with the original, tends to ultimately approximate the interlinear version, and greatly simplifies the apprehension of the original; we thereby find ourselves in a sense brought back to the primitive text, and thus the circle in which the transition from the foreign to the native, from the known to the unknown takes place is finally closed."[32] Goethe calls for this third type of translation, and it took the entire poetic genius of Goethe to give Orientalism a nobility of thought and a poetic dwelling turned toward the beauty of the other. Goethe bases Orientalism on the roots of Being, and his *Divan* is well worth almost all of Berque's works.

Indeed, apart from a few very rare specialized and often dubious efforts, Arabic poetry still awaits its translators. Berque in his own manner helps point the way and this is the greatest significance of his work. But we must first clarify the issue of what he calls heterophony. It refers, for instance, to Arab authors who write in French, in particular: "Without wishing to be indiscreet, let us say that it is not normal for an avant-garde of Arab literature, poetry included, to be expressed in the language of the other. Has this not resulted in an expatriation of the inside? It is only too true."[33] Precisely, the question must be raised, since in question is a linguistic simulacrum that is borne also by the bilingual desire of Orientalism, but in an opposite sense. Mirror plays: the professional Orientalist finds himself in conflict, in his own language, with a dangerous contender who in a way tends to occupy the same place, the same stage. We implicitly understand the share of mutual resentment that stimulates this sort of debate. It is essential here to designate the question in its own terms, beyond Berque's psychological and tactical formulation. The being of a language is turned toward the one who goes toward it, toward the one who—in himself—radically inscribes himself in the interval between identity and difference. This interval is the scene of the text, what it puts at stake. In Maghrebi literature, such an interval—when it becomes text and poem—imposes itself through its radical strangeness, in other words, through a writing that seeks its roots in another language, in an absolute outside. How to measure what may happen in this radical strangeness? If our desire is basically bilingual, in the name of what will Berque keep us from responding to him in his own language and outside his stilted rhetoric?

In Berque's books, the Arabs have taken the path of clandestinity, like the Maghrebi emigrants in Barbès, which is consistent with the refined and sophisticated logic of his approach. For—and this is a paradox for an Orientalist—Jacques Berque does not love Islam; he loves pre-Islam. A perfectly legitimate love, but why does he delude himself about the places of his desire? He celebrates the *Jahiliyya* and its poetry with such intensity and such naturalistic and paganistic nostalgia that we readily give both ears (Islamic and pre-Islamic) to what he has to say: "The only reason I speak of ancient poetry is my love for ancient Arabic poetry."[34] This love does not renew the question of Orientalism, but the way in which Berque translates some *Mu'allaqāt* (pre-Islamic poems) is of a silken, almost singing style, filled with assonances à la Saint-John Perse. Something intimate and essential is revealed in this crepuscular man who spends his time writing boring and phony books in order to hide from himself. What he says—with an entirely literary feeling—of the inarticulate origin of the message of the Quran and what he notes with a muscular lightness on the being of poetry or on the ruins lost in the Bedouin desert are a reminder of the decadent mirages of the East, sung in the minor key of a certain Volney, before the pharaonic ruins. With Napoleon, Orientalism entered the imperialism of Absolute Knowledge. With Berque, it rediscovers the nostalgic fantasy of its disappearance.

Exergue II

In a noble sense, the Orientalist is the one who watches over the dawn of thought—a proposition not to be considered as an appropriate metaphor, but as the idea of a radical position. The East and the West are not reduced to a geographical distribution or to some cultural difference. But they call, in their spacing, every cardinal question of Being, according to an auroral and nuptial protocol—a protocol that does not refer to some illuminative philosophy that would come to transfigure, through a solar imagery, the unthought-of birth of all East and all West. This birth dictates the song of the awakening. And as such, it is always an extraordinary event. It is never given as a supernatural gift from heaven. As gift, as distraught memory, this birth celebrates the unthought. Distraught memory, insofar as the gift, brings an intoxicated moment between the companions. But for such a gift to give itself in the proximity of the other, it too must be realized according to a thought of difference.

Radical Orientalism. Perhaps the question of the Far East is by itself extreme, disproportionate compared to the Greco-Arab issue here mentioned—extreme in that it is a promise. But the Far East is not supernatural; it receives in its own way the one who marches toward it, the one who has always gone toward it. Also we should not wait indefinitely to start again the dialogue. The imperial globality of technology may not herald the event of a homonymous thought, distinctly sheltered in the Same. It can, on the contrary, ensure an enslavement never seen before.

In his wonderful poem (*West-East Divan*) of a pure freedom, Goethe shows us the way:

Occident and Orient alike
Offer you pure things to taste.
Leave there the fancies, and leave the peel,
Sit down to the great feast:
You wouldn't want to, even in passing,
Despise this meal.[35]
Who knows himself and others well
No longer may ignore:
Occident and Orient dwell
Separately no more.[36]

References

We did not want to encumber this chapter with repetitive references. We therefore refer the reader to Berque's book and to the countless citations that justify our reading. We have arranged these citations in line with the dominant themes of the book.

(1976)

4

Sexuality according to the Quran

In a foregoing passage we wrote, "Let us not forget that Islam *veils* the face of women too, since the *houris* cannot be seen *here below* except in the mystical paradise, isn't it so? That is to say, in a hallucination of the visible? Thus, within this hierarchy of the visible and the invisible, woman is placed between God and man; visible invisible, she is the *mise en abyme* of the theological order. Who ever kept you from working in this direction?" (cf. Chapter 1.)

Yes, we shall try to work in this direction.[1]

A few remarks have to be made before we move on to our discussion. These remarks are necessary when we think about the extreme shyness and the prudential silence of Maghrebi (and Arab) researchers regarding what is called "sexuality." A tacit question, which should itself be analyzed as such, especially as the Islamic religion encourages us to raise it: "There is no shyness[2] in religion," says a *hadith* often cited by jurists and theologians. Also, we are taking these prophetic words literally, as we have done before,[3] but in a transtheological approach, allowing us to concentrate on the superposition of the metaphysical plane and the social plane, the place of the exchange of women.

Sexuality? Sexuality in Islam? As a notion, "sexuality" is quite recent. It dates from the mid-nineteenth century, belonging already to an entirely determined discursive set in the field of Western civilization. This dating is open to speculation, but the important thing is to underline first of all the emergence of this *scienta sexualis* that Michel Foucault talks about—a science that consists in telling the truth of sex. The same philosopher makes the following warning: "An endeavor that does not date from the nineteenth century, even if it was then that a nascent science lent it a singular form. It was the basis of all the aberrant, naïve and cunning discourses where knowledge of sex seems to have strayed for such a long time."[4]

To talk of "sexuality" in Islam is from the outset to carry out an act of translation from one language to another, from one civilization to another. The important thing in this act is to specify, in the first place, the use of the notions and concepts put into question, to identify the effects of their transformation, so that "sexuality"—sign and thing—is returned to speech that can say it, and to the body that joins it.

Now, in the Arabic language, the language of the Quran and therefore of the primordial discourse on sexuality in Islam,[5] there is no unique concept or notion that bears this name, which would be the formulation of a domain reserved to sex. There is rather a web of notions, which jurisprudence and dogmatic theology have tried to contain with the notion of *nikah* [conjunction, marriage], to which we shall come back later. However, we can already affirm that this reduction of the sexual question to its marital, familial, procreative, and patriarchal function will be treated here as the enunciator of a discourse, the discourse of the law (*sharia*) on and around sex, and not as its "truth" or rather its reality, which has always been polymorphous and multiple in its effects of manifestation and simulation.

We need to come to an understanding on this point, that is, we need to understand this: sexuality in Islam *and* Islam according to sexuality. A crossed relationship between two orders of discourse—and of their disorder.

In a study, a Tunisian researcher called Tahar Labib, already in the first chapter, raises the issue of the relationship between sexuality and the Arabic language: "In the ethics of Islam, language—in both senses of the word—and sex are strongly linked."[6] *Lisan*, as language and as the organ of the tongue, a double sense to be indexed by sex! This researcher insists on the "sexual segregation" that marks the grammar, rhetoric, and poetry of the Arabic language—a very questionable assertion, to which we shall come back.

He also notes the particular case of the *tadādd* (or *al-addād*) [opposition, contradiction], which is a homonymy of contraries and characterizes the archaism of the Semitic languages—a homonymy that has greatly intrigued classical Arab grammarians and has aroused the equally "Semitic" curiosity of Freud regarding the ambivalence of the word being spoken in a logic of opposition, a thwarted manifestation of Eros, if we accept that Freud wanted to differentiate sex and Eros: "What psychoanalysis calls sexuality," he writes, "was by no means identical with the impulsion toward a union of the two sexes or toward producing a pleasurable sensation in the genitals; it had far more resemblance to the all-inclusive and all-embracing love of Plato's *Symposium*."[7] In short, this is the whole metaphysical story of love in the West. We are simply signaling it here, with no intention of developing it further.

Anyhow, the case of the *tadādd* is rare in the corpus of the Arabic language. And in any event, this exception, this apparent aberration of the logic of sense does not structure the whole of the language. More generally, a language is not its grammar, its rhetoric, or its poetry. It is neither masculine nor feminine, neither maternal nor paternal. Language is neutral and impersonal.

Labib recalls the following words of the theologian Ibn Malik: "The noun is in principle masculine. The feminine is a branch (which recalls the image of Eve created from Adam's rib). And since gender is the origin, the masculine noun has no need of a sign indicating its gender. As to the feminine gender, which is a branch, it needs a sign that indicates it, such as the *ta*."[8] The researcher does not refer here to a concept of language, but to a theo-grammatical fiction of the origin, of the Adamic separation and the sign, through divine creation: metaphor through which the woman—supplement of the body and the name of man—is constituted as an *adornment* of masculine desire.

Those who would like to rejoice in it can read the following sentence gathered in the encyclopedic work of Yaqut al-Hamawi (1179–1229): "The adornment of men is the Arabic language; that of women, opulence [*sic*]."[9] Besides, the Quran does not exactly confirm such an assertion: "They (women) are clothing for you and you are clothing for them; ... dwell with them and seek what Allah prescribes for you" (Surah *The Cow*, 183–187).[10]

From the Quran to dogmatic theology and jurisprudence, the logic of the adornment is indeed rather twisted. Often, theology retains from the preceding verses the first element of the metaphor (the adornment) by veiling the opposite and complementary movement of desire—that of the double adornment—through which the body veiling and unveiling itself is an addressing to the other.

The theologies of Islam, its knowledges and mysticisms, are therefore particular readings of the Quran, which are historically, politically, and culturally situated with regard to the law of the text that they interpret, and comment on by framing it according to their ideological framework and their mode of deciphering.

The same is true for grammar and rhetoric. The example analyzed by Labib (*dakar*, sabre and sexual organ, and *'untā*, female, as well as all the derivations he opposes almost term by term) does not constitute, by itself, a global opposition of the Arabic language, a sexual segregation that would be inherent to it. The fact that sexual difference is named by different signifiers is one of the laws of language, which is Difference—but that this researcher transforms this difference into an opposition, or rather into a linguistic sexual segregation, is what reproduces the metaphysics of grammatical categories as generator matrix of the language faculty, of language [*la langue*[11]], and of the symbolic.

This is an untenable position, the place where we try to identify the sacrifice of women between, on the one hand, theology and jurisprudence, and on the other, the sublimation of the mystical and aesthetic Eros, which makes the woman's body the pomp of a beautiful poem or of an annihilation—and without intermediaries—in the love of God—trance of the ascetic freed from all bodily attachment.

But we shall not address all these issues of mysticism. Let us now focus our attention on the Quran.

Yes, to read and reread the Quran according to an other-thought.[12] This means, first of all, that we are putting in parentheses the entire immense archive of glosses and exegeses about and on the basis of the Quran. This is a tenable position, to the extent that our reading will be *logically* convincing for every reader—believer or not. Therefore, we will be rereading the Quran, excluding the *hadith*. This prophetic word, intermediary between the divine word and men, raises huge problems of interpretation, which we are currently unable to resolve, in the present stage of our research.

We choose the Quranic perspective itself, about "sexuality," without making explicit reference (or very rarely) to other monotheistic texts.

We begin with the Quran and with the question of naming—a necessary detour on the unnamed feminine.

In creating the universe, Allah inaugurates existence by naming. The name is at the very foundation of creation, the sign that edifies the existent, every existent in its introduction to the world, according to the cycle of double life and double death. This process of naming, which is all over the Quran, makes the created into a palimpsest, for to Allah is due—from him to him—the act of naming and erasing.

Palimpsest. The status of languages is double; by giving different languages to the peoples, Allah introduces, in the same act, a founding difference to the very concept of creation of languages. This difference is between the Arabic language revealed in a "Clear Book" (*Kitabun Mubeen*) and the other languages. This difference institutes Islam in *one* language such that the Idea of the One (and of Islamic monotheism) and the oneness of language are strictly solidary as sacral message, which is, simultaneously and paradoxically, a particular and universal message—particular as language and universal as message.

This is why, when we name Islam, when we talk or write on Islam (like I am doing right here), it is always a matter of *translating* this principial indissociability of the One and of absolute unity: "Say: He is Allah the One. Allah The Only One. He neither begets nor is begotten. He has no equal"[13] (Surah *The Unity, Sincerity, Oneness of Allah*). No anthropomorphism then, no "association" of whatever kind with Allah, no trinitary figure either. The One is the One, united with himself, in the name that bears him and is borne by him. And this name of the One is the creator of every naming.

Along comes Adam. Adam is the first of the names of men, the inaugural name and the *aleph* of the Semitic alphabets: A. First letter of the first name, the first proper name, and at the same time, Adam is the first mediator named between Allah and every naming. And Eve—let us not forget—was never thus designated in the Quran. *The first woman is unnamed.*

Between the One and the first man, there is no genealogy, no filiation, and no resemblance. There is absolute separation between Allah and men. And to this first man, Allah gives naming itself. Let us cite from the Quran: "And Allah taught Adam all the names"[14] (Surah *The Cow*, 30). It is about names, and not words—would the name then be at the very foundation of the word? And conversely, would the word be a supplement, an adornment of the name? Where does their difference occur in the act of creating languages? We are leaving these questions open. For what interests us is the relation of naming and unnaming between the two sexes.

Second moment. Adam says to the Angels what Allah has taught him: It seems that this word *mala'ika*, in Arabic, is the broken plural of a Canaanite word. I quote,

> And He taught Adam all the names, then He showed all those who bear those names to the Angels, and He said to the Angels: "Tell me the names of these beings if you are truthful.—Glory to You! We have no knowledge except what You have taught us. You, You are the all-knowing, the wise."[15] (Surah *The Cow*, 29–32)

We talk of the angel further below. Let us continue our commentary, with no reference to any explicit doctrine. Let us continue to read the text, on the basis of the Adamic narrative, and where the (Christian) notion of sin proves overloaded, a translation/treason of the very notion of sexuality in Islam, in its own symbolic field.

The Adamic narrative thus begins by naming; then it shows the prostration of the Angels before Adam, who is capable of repeating the names, of naming in his turn, and of engaging in the process of naming.

Now this introduction to the name is itself introduction to the Garden and to its homonym, Paradise. Science, Propaedeutic to the Garden of Paradise. Here we are closely following this synonymy in the

Arabic language. What language will the believers speak in paradise? This question, long discussed among theologians, will not be discussed here, because on the one hand the Quran was revealed in Arabic, and on the other, there is no mention of the language of paradise, which leaves the problem unresolved.

Homonymic introduction, then, to the metaphor of the Garden of Paradise, through the naming of Adam, while Eve remains unnamed. At this point, the issue is raised of *jouissance*,[16] of seduction by Iblis. Let us quote the text translated by Blachère, crossing out the notion of sin:

> "O Adam!" said Allah, "tell us the names. And when Adam had told the Angels the names, Allah said: "Did I not tell you that I know the Unknowable of heaven and earth and that I know what you make manifest and what you keep secret?" And when we said: "O Adam! dwell you and your spouse in this garden. Eat thereof with pleasure and delight, where you will. Approach not this tree, or you will be among the Unjust."
>
> Then the devil drew them away from the Garden; he made them leave the state they had been in and we said: "Go down. You will be enemies with one another. You will have upon the earth a place of settlement and provision[17] [*jouissance*] for a time."[18] (*The Cow*, 29–36)

The Quran does not explicitly mention sin (*dhanb*, *ithm*, etc.), but rather infidelity, injustice toward the self, and "being away from the Garden." This changes the notion of sin. It is between the separation from the Garden of Paradise (eternal state of bliss) and the ephemeral felicity of here below, between the Adamic power of naming and the rebellion of Iblis, that the text must be read, and without the Old or New Testament with commentary and translation in between. Thus, there is no original sin or fall, but an act of disobedience that is explicitly avowed by Iblis and assumed by him.

This reading is strictly consistent with the text. We can verify its effects and implications in order to mark the difference of the notions at play in the surah *Al-A'raf* [*The Heights*]:

> "O Adam! dwell you and your spouse in this Garden. Eat wherever you will. Approach not this tree, or you will be among the Unjust."

But Iblis made a suggestion to them, to make apparent to them that which was concealed in their nakedness. He said to them: "Your Lord has only forbidden you to touch these fruit that you may not become Angels or Immortals." He lured them thus. When they tasted the fruit from the tree, what was concealed of their nakedness appeared to them. Their Lord called unto to them: "Did I not forbid you (to approach) that tree? Did I not tell you that Satan is your avowed enemy?"

"—Our Lord," replied Adam and his spouse. "We have wronged ourselves, and if You do not forgive us and have mercy upon us, we shall be among the Losers."

He replied to them: "Go down! You are enemies to one another. You will have on the earth a place of settlement and enjoyment [*jouissance*] for a term appointed."

The Lord said: "On the earth you shall live, and there you shall die, and from it you shall be brought back."

O Sons of Adam! We have sent down to you clothing that conceals what is concealed by your nakedness, as well as garments. But the adornment of piety is best; these are the signs of Allah, so that you may take heed.

O Sons of Adam, let not Satan lure you as he did your father and mother.[19]

It is important to underline the word *waswasa* (root: *wasa*)—to inspire perverse things, to insinuate devilry (*al-waswas*, one of the attributes of Satan), but also to become delusional. The notion of "madness" in Islam cannot be grasped if we do not refer to possession by an evil spirit, which is at once the demonic factor, the tempter, and that which leads to delusion. Otherwise, how to understand the very notion of Satan, or Iblis, and the transition here from an eternal state of bliss in the Garden to an ephemeral felicity?

What Satan says—about nakedness, in view of nakedness—is an inversion, a perversion of the prohibition. Satan says to Adam and his companion: God forbids you from seeing your nakedness to prevent you from achieving otherworldliness or immortality. He forbids you from being yourselves, that is, free beings, capable of disobedience, like

I am. Satan argues with Allah about transgression. For, as transgressor, he has to carry out his mission of wrongdoing and seduction. He has to accept the law while being outside the law. Satanic logic is to maintain this contradiction, this perversion of the law, which means that Satan plays the role of anti-prophet, seducer of men, and not that of anti-Allah. But this he cannot do in the logic of the Quran. Just as the prophet must ensure justice, obedience, and adoration of Allah, in the same way, and by inversion, the Satanic apparatus must sow the seeds of transgression. His duty is given and given to him by Allah, and Iblis takes charge of this duty as such. Now, the error of Adam and Eve is an *injustice* that they commit against themselves and against future humanity. Not a mistake, a sin, but an injustice—this difference is essential. Error and loss (*al-khasireen*) are, at the very foundation of Islamic morality, a primordial division, a separation from the self to the self introduced by Satan and always under his threat. Hence the instability of *jouissance*, that disorder inherent to the body, and which the Muslim is constantly called to exorcize through purification and all the required ritual.

There is contradiction between Satan and men, since creation itself, in the naming of the world, and in the very substance of the body— human body "created from clay" and body of Iblis, created from fire. These two principles, which should not be confused with the dualism of Manichaeism, are principles of an ethical separation, through which the metaphor (of fire and earth) is not defined in relation to a naturalistic metaphysics, but to a higher exigency of the One, the principle of principles. We may say of the One that he has no association, no double, no shadow, and no simulacrum. The one, and not one—in other words, a name, and not a number. It cannot be associated with three either, as in the Trinity. The big error is precisely to introduce an "association" to the concept of Allah, in its absolute unity—according to the Quran. All we are doing is commenting.

Allah creates birth and death; he creates resurrection; he creates the father and his name, the father of all men (Adam) and their mother (the unnamed) and their children. He creates everything, without any intermediary between him and his creatures. No anthropomorphism, we had said, no genealogy, and no filiation. It is a crazy idea—according to the Quran—to believe that from three comes the One! And if I quickly recall this—moreover extremely remarkable—idea of the Trinity, it is that the (Christian) earthly family is based upon the concept of the Holy Family. But it may be objected that Islam must explain the concept of triad (natural, symbolic, Oedipal, as you wish), and therefore the position of the child. Yes, but there is no transition from the One to the three. What is an Islamic child?

Allah created from a single being (*nafs*) Adam and his unnamed spouse. The noun *nafs*, of feminine gender, has several connotations: spirit, soul, evil eye, blood, body. There is also a whole series of expressions, for instance: *nafs al-shay'*, the core/the essence of a thing. To cite another example, he himself came (*nafsuhu*). In short, etymologically, this word conveys in itself the idea of being, at once corporeal and spiritual.

The unnamed Eve would be derived from this being that precedes her, but she was already there. She is within Adam as *nafs*, and then she separates herself from him, detaches herself in difference. Also note that there is no separation between the conception of the child and his absolute and total creation by Allah. Creation and procreation obey the same law. Allah creates the child in the woman's body, leaving him to his destiny, which is the cycle of double life and double death. Thus, the child is born in accordance with this cycle: he dies, then he lives, then he dies, then he rises again, turning to Allah.

Let us take the liberty of interpreting this our own way. Allah is always the Great Other, the absolutely different Other, difference itself. It is this radical separation that should be understood when an Islamic child is born: he is not born as an identity engendered by the union of two other identities or by the couple's will to procreate, but always and already through the cycle of double life and double death—a circle where the child turns to Allah; and if he dies soon after birth, he will fly to heaven as tradition has it. As a consequence, he is not born as union of the man and woman, but rather in the form of a palimpsest, as one moment of a cycle or a circle—he is an imprint of it. Then how to think love in this radical separation between Allah and men?

We shall come back to this question. But before that, it is necessary to refer again and again to the Abrahamic narrative—narrative that remains exemplary in this case, in this relationship between the father and the son. We have noted elsewhere[20] how the question of Abraham in the Quranic text has been transformed.

On one side, the sacrifice of his son is told in a dream. And it is the father who tells the son this dream of sacrifice. The son obeys and accepts his sacrifice by divine order. The child sees and therefore imagines himself killed in the paternal dream. He realizes both the will of Allah and the thwarted desire of his father. The son does not belong to the father; it is not a relationship of consanguinity that binds them, but a relation of equality before God, in total submission. An equality of expropriation—the father does not have a right of ownership and of appropriation on the son. He is the father of a son who should not return to him.

On the one hand, we had said that the father dreams that his son is sacrificed, and at his own hands. Murder that is not a murder, not only because it is merely dreamed (and there will be much to say about this dream by reversing the Freudian Oedipus hypothesis), but also because by thus making the father dream, Allah shows him the limits of the law. On the other hand, this is not a law that binds the father to the son, the son to the father, but a principle of law that is its own law and the end of all law. Abraham is caught at this intersection of filial love and the requirement of a sacrifice. He must separate himself from himself and his son, be torn in his paternity, divide himself, and kill his own offspring to rise to God's unshakable order. There is something incomprehensible, something terribly disconcerting there for Abraham (and for every father).[21] But if we read the Quran from cover to cover, tracing this exigency of the One, we can find ourselves faced with an implacable logic.

And this logic of the sacrifice relates to the superhumanity of the concept of the One, and not to the filial relation in its humanity, blood,

family, clan, tribe, and genealogy. For the One to achieve its complete
autonomy and transcendence, it is necessary to exclude all "association"
with Allah, and human association itself; the couple, the man, the
woman, and the child are all placed in a union sacrificed to Allah—
union without union: again the palimpsest.

Let us recapitulate: If we have chosen this chronology by going all
the way back to Adam, it is because this is the chronology of creation
as it enunciates itself. We begin with the beginning of this primordial
distinction between God and men, body and mind, man and woman,
and the demonic and the heavenly—the founding oppositions of
(Islamic) monotheism.

There is still a hopeless metaphysical war between man and
woman: either man considers himself prior to woman and the closest
to God, or, by inversion, woman in turn thinks herself the natural
beginning of every child, and therefore of every man. But precisely,
in Islam, there is no symbolic break between the principle of creation
and procreation. Allah is the Great Other that has no beginning and
no end. On the other hand, as we have said repeatedly, the relationship
between man and woman must follow the cycle of double life and
double death.

It is this circularity that we have in mind with this somewhat rotating
chronology. This rotation is also that of the narratives described in the
corpus of the Quran, in a form at times identical and at others more or
less different—such is the narrative of Adam, that of Abraham, Joseph,
and Muhammad himself. The important thing is not to reconstruct
this or that story to tell it again ourselves, but the symbolic stakes of
what goes on around what we would call "sexuality in Islam," as if my
body, in rereading the Quran, had to reproduce its Islamic truth by
transposing it—reproduction, which we vouch for, on our own behalf,
and beyond all doctrine.

We shall begin again with the beauty of an angelic prophet.

The narrative of Joseph. When his master had bought him in Egypt,
he was perhaps thinking of taking him as an adopted child. Adoption
between whom and whom? Between what and what?

Before we answer, let us focus on the scenography of the seduction, which is so admirable. The question of this seduction might be posed in the following manner: can a woman love an adopted child as angelic prophet? Yes, thinks the master's wife. She draws him toward her desire, offering him to make love to her. She tells him, "Come! I am yours." But an angel is an apparition that does not give itself. An angel awakens desire by disappointing it. It drives mad and makes delirious. The angel is an ecstasy and not a sex. And he can only refuse what the woman wants from him. In order to become her adopted son, and not her lover, Joseph must maintain his prophetic and angelic distance; he must preserve his devastating beauty in order to free her from his sexuality. There is, in this troubling and ambivalent scene, the simulacrum of a suspended incest, a "false" adoption that this woman wants to use in her favor—her own. The ruse of this seductress is: you may perhaps be my husband's adopted child, but you shall first be my lover.

Then what *Zuleika* (this is her name according to tradition, but this name does not exist in the Quran: she too is unnamed) loves about Yusuf (Joseph), what draws her irresistibly toward transgression is indeed his legendary beauty, but it is also this extraordinary temptation to seduce an angelic prophet, to sexualize him, to give him a body, and to give herself to herself in a way both as woman and as falsely adoptive and incestuous mother; in short, she tends to immoralize desire and give it over to its obscenity.

Joseph is indeed attracted to her, but he does not give in, yet ... yet he is about to give in when he remembers the "teachings of God": limit where desire, just when it is about to be quenched, is all of a sudden retained, and suspended by the voice of Allah. Maddening limit where, having lost their heads, the angelic prophet and his seductress have to consume the prohibited pleasure solely in "spirit." The body stops—petrification, and two statues of stone. Let us resume.

In this scene, the expression *wa-rāwadthou an-nafihi* repeats several times—an expression often avoided by commentators and translators in its crudest connotation: to try to have sexual intercourse with someone. And here "she" is the one doing the trying. This straightforward meaning is confirmed by the encyclopedic dictionary *Lisān al-ʿArab*. Good. But whether sexuality is permitted or suspended, prohibited or tolerated, it has to be laid bare in a scene of sexuality. For the law to hit and suspend desire, you need the ruses of seduction, you need a perversion, a perverse outsider, an immoral, shameless, and therefore obscene will. This is the meaning of the presence of Satan between man and woman.

But Joseph is a prophet, in other words, a man honored by God, in yet other words, a man of angelic and charismatic qualities. God speaks when unbridled passion must be brought back to law and order. But for the seduction to take place, for Satan to be able to intervene in the confusion of the body and especially the feminine body (both human and demonic), Allah maintains at all times the possibility of a proof. Suspension of the scene when Joseph's shirt is torn from behind by Zuleika. Impossibility of rape by a woman, yes of course, and the rape of an angelic prophet moreover, yes again; but in this violent gesture and in this madness, it is also a flight of Joseph, a diversion of his desire, a separation from him to him. It all happens as if Joseph were a woman, moreover a woman incapable of giving herself. It can be said that he plays the role of a woman so that the inversion of man and woman becomes the parade of an impossible seduction. At no time does he attempt to seduce Zuleika; he is tempted by her, forced by her to go against his prophethood, his angelism, and his problematic adoption—in short, to fall into the obscenity of his hidden sex. She is the one who acts, plays tricks, accuses, lies, feigns truth and error, and elaborates the scene of seduction. She forgets herself by forgetting God and her own husband. Adultery—with an adopted son—is a double transgression, that of the lawful relationships and that of a devilry, a madness of loving without (moral) reason. Passion—and we are still commenting—is an error, a demonic whispering, satanic revolt, and ruse of feminine seduction.

The third moment of this scene also describes the apparition of an angel:

30. In town, women said: "The Master's wife wants to seduce [*coïter*] her servant. She is infatuated by him. The truth is we indeed see her in manifest error."

31. When she heard of their scheming, she sent for them, had oranges prepared for them, and gave each one of them a knife. "Come out before them," she ordered Joseph. When the women saw him, they found him so beautiful that they cut their hands, and exclaimed: "God forbid! This is no mortal. This is a noble archangel."²² (Surah *Joseph*)

Ruse against ruse: it is Zuleika who makes an apparition appear. She acts out her own possession, by provoking a trance. She also comes "in spirit," embarrassing Joseph in his dazzling beauty, and at the same time she becomes the queen of the scene, seduction itself. A cruel game. To release himself, Joseph turns to God.

What this narrative shows is that woman is sacrificed between adultery and seduction. Seducing an angelic prophet, losing her mind, and using cunning with this madness make woman the being who is the closest to Satan. That is why woman is madness when she does not obey this sacrifice.

Interlude. Let us recall this mysterious passage of the Quran where we see the famous Queen of Sheba undergo a real hallucination before submitting to the word of Allah—scene to be found in the surah *The Ant, The Ants*. We will make a brief comment on this passage of hallucination.

The other character is Solomon who had learned the language (*mantiq*) of the birds. There he is heading for the idolatrous people of Sheba, commanding armies of jinn, mortal men, and birds. A jinni brings him the queen's throne in the blink of an eye. Solomon orders that the throne be disguised. When she sees the throne, the queen says, "How it looks like it."²³ Necessary substitution in order to prove that the "magnificent throne" is due to Allah, and that that of the queen is a demonic ruse! It is not the object itself (the idol) that is the symbol of power, but the ability to make it appear and disappear instantaneously, to transform it into a sign given by Allah. And since Allah commands also the rotation of the sun (worshipped by the Sabaeans), he shows this people that such an object is a lure, a pure appearance, a natural phenomenon empty in itself. Allah is invisible, and the worship of the visible is therefore always an act of fetishization, an iconolatry. That is why the queen must undergo a kind of initiation in the strange form of a hallucination, a spiritual rapture. Her throne is disguised, made unrecognizable, or rather hardly recognizable in this transition from fetish to sign, from fetish to metaphor, from iconolatry to the worship of the invisible One.

Let us reread this cryptic verse:

> They said to her (the queen): "Enter the palace." When she saw it, she thought it was a pool of water and bared her calves. Solomon said: "It is a palace paved with crystal."[24]

Hallucination, substituting one fetish for another (the calves), that moment through which the queen's foot remains suspended in the narrative, between the illusion of water and the appearance of the crystal, matter that is in itself a transparency, a form of simulacrum. It is this simulation that Allah shows in order to confuse the malicious mind of Satan and therefore that of the queen. He turns around, reverses the powers of illusion. The queen then enters into belief, as if in a waking dream through an association of substitutive images. And through this substitution she shows a bit of her nudity. Why this detail, precisely? If we allow ourselves to make a quick interpretation of this suspension of the foot and this little bit of nudity between the water and the crystal, we would say that what arrests the power of illusion (considered here as idolatry) is the diversion of the appearances by an infinite play of simulacra in the hands of God. Only the belief in God, says the Quran, blocks illusion in its destructive power. He is the truth that plays with and on illusion, at his own discretion: It is not that a woman seduces God.

In order to better situate the position of "sexuality" in Islam, we should consider sexual difference as secondary in relation to the difference between belief and unbelief, between the absolute exigency of the One and its "association" with any trinity, with other gods, and other pagan cults. The One is the Only One.

Sexual difference will be taken and understood as a social rule, a law of exchange governed by a strict calculation of the licit and the illicit. Whether it is called tribal, patriarchal, polygamous, or segregate, Islamic society as enunciated in the Quran is first of all metaphysical before being worldly; or more exactly, it is moral because it is metaphysical, following the cycle of double life and double death. But we shall see that between metaphysics and the societal, the same circularity is at work. The juxtaposition of two planes in difference. That is our hypothesis.

That is why attention must be paid first to the metaphysical hierarchy in order to identify the relationship between men and women. A first fundamental question would be: what is the prophet Muhammad's place in this hierarchy? As both prophet and man, Muhammad is not the father of the believing men and women; he is simply a "messenger." In this sense, Muslims are orphaned of the symbolic Father, whereas the prophet's wives are their mothers. Strictly speaking, there is no triad, no trinity in the Christian or Freudian sense:

- Muhammad is the father of none of your males, but he is the apostle of Allah and the Seal of the Prophets.[25]
- The prophet is closer to the Believers than they are to themselves. His spouses are their mothers. Those bound by blood relations are closer to one another, in the book of Allah, than the other Believers and Emigrants.[26]
- Provided, however, that you do what is deemed right to your friends: that is inscribed in the Book (Cf. Surah *The Clans, The Coalition, The Combined Forces*).[27]

The Prophet's wives are forbidden to the other Muslims: no one can marry them, take the Prophet's place, succeed him, and replace his line by mixing it. Rupture between the symbolic image of the father and that of the mother: the believer is a fatherless child, while Allah is the Only One.

There are at least two categories of women: those of the Prophet and the others. And because they "are not like any of the other women"[28] (Surah *The Clans, The Coalition, The Combined Forces*, 32) and their difference is a privilege, which makes them at once the wives of the Prophet and the (symbolic) mothers of the believing men and women, the Prophet's wives are the model of what is licit and illicit between the two sexes. What the Prophet asks them to do is not to adorn themselves and show themselves off, and therefore play the game of seduction. No, what he requires of them is that they believe in God and in himself, by keeping away from all turpitude: "Allah only wishes to remove all impurity from you! O Members of the House (of the Prophet)!, and He wishes to purify you completely"[29] (Surah *The Clans, The Coalition, The Combined Forces*, 33).

But if the Prophet's wives are prohibited to the others (believers), the Prophet can marry any free believer—in addition to his wives—slaves of war, and *cousines filles* of the Emigrants. In this respect, we know the story of the Prophet and Zaynab, the wife of his adopted son Zayd. The prophet had desired this woman. Zayd repudiated her. It had taken a special revelation on this issue to show the Prophet that his marriage to Zaynab was lawful and that a son must not be confused with an adopted son. Remember the story of Joseph and compare the two narratives.

There is no incest and no semblance of incest in marrying the wife of one's adopted son, provided that their sexual relations end. Adoption does not equal blood relationship. The adopted child remains always an other: I cannot pretend having begotten him, and he has to keep the name of his real father. There can be no confusion between the two lines and the two names. To the adopted child I can only give my protection, help, and assistance, and he is sexually my equal. The adopted child no longer has a father, he is orphaned of his father, and he can only become father in his turn. He is always a founder and not a pure simulacrum; he is beyond the dead father. He has to always separate himself and break with his adoptive parents, being already separated from his real parents. It is this double separation that makes the destiny of adoption. And there is, according to the Quran, no paradox in this principle of circularity: I repudiate my wife that my adoptive parent marries in his turn. Each will bear the name of their line. And the woman will be this intersection between two names, the chiasmus that binds the two men—by dividing them.

This is the message delivered to us about Zaynab.

The other narrative we shall deal with is that of Aisha, the young bride, Muhammad's favorite. Such a prophet can of course only be deceived by God (when God wants to put him to the test), but never by his wives (even when they wish to do so). What deceives is the lies of others. For instance, the story of Aisha. Before leaving for the battle of *Banu Al-Mustaliq* (626 CE), Muhammad cast lots as he always did to determine who among his wives should accompany him, and the lot fell on Aisha. On the way back from this triumphant battle, Aisha was lost from sight for an indefinite time. She would later say that she had lost her necklace, which was the reason for her being late. The Prophet and his companions noticed that she was late and waited for a certain time. She arrived, says tradition, sitting behind a young camel driver. This event caused a big stir and became a political story.

A revelation came to bring order (cf. Surah *Light*), confirming that this was a satanic calumny, a "great slander"[30] (*buhtan*), an infamy because not based on the testimony of the four people present. The law of retaliation will then be applied not only in this world, but also in the next, in hell. But let us note that such a heavenly law of retaliation is not always intractable: it is always up to God to erase the error. His justice decides; and as such, obeying no human criteria, this justice is unknowable. All that turns to and is due to God is just, on principle.

Aisha's adultery is impossible. Not because she was not capable of failing (she is a woman), but because her adultery is inconceivable. Otherwise, this would have been a demonic error, a victory of Iblis over the prophet, and therefore an impurity of his line, an impure stain in his charismatic genealogy. The Prophet's wives are sacrosanct—no jinni, no mortal can seduce them, and seduce the prohibition by a reversal of alliance, or rather by a confusion of alliance between prophecy and Satanism. For the soul to reach up to heaven, for it to deserve paradise, there must be an absolute purification of sexuality—not a sublimation, but purification. But we shall come back to this heaven, the *houris*, and the eternal state of bliss in the end.

Such are the two major marital conflicts in the earthly life of Muhammad.

Let us finally address the structure of the system.

First, the notion of *nikah*—a notion marked by a certain wavering, at times sexual intercourse, fornication, at others marital sexual relationship. This latter sense is more prevalent in general, while the word *wata'* is reserved for sexual intercourse per se and brings to mind the image of a trampling on, stepping on, and riding (a horse, and by extension, a woman)—in a word, a metaphor for sexual equitation. There is a very rich vocabulary that designates, in Arabic, the act of love. What interests us here is the hierarchy of the metaphysical and the societal in the idea of Islam itself. In the cycle of double life and double death, there is principial equality in belief, regardless of sexual difference: the One is the One, beyond all difference.

Equality, which is obviously dissymmetrical between the two sexes, but symmetrical on the level of the system and theory, to the extent that the circle of exchange completes the metaphysical circle, and vice versa. Reversibility from the one to the other—morality is the theorization of this.

Governed by the exchange of women, the social system is a system of absolute circularity. What is important is not an opposition between monogamy and polygamy, but a permutational and serial mating, in accordance with the very specific rules of marriage, repudiation, and remarriage. It is not so much love, but rather justice that must govern this circularity. Dogmatic theology and jurisprudence have been the sciences and codifications of these permutational laws. The important thing is not the concept of man or woman as such, but the principle of a circular classification. And if we must talk of difference between the two sexes, let us say that it is inherent, logically and metaphysically, to the whole system. For this system to function, there must be structural circularity between the metaphysical plane and the societal plane; for it to circulate precisely, there is need to obey not only rules of exchange but also a requirement of justice, a morality. This is a more or less happy justice, according to God's will; it is happy if the code of rules is respected. It does not matter that I can marry one, two, three, or four women and have a few concubines; what matters is that I try to be impartial. My chances of success, my salvation here below and in the hereafter, do not eventually depend on the number of my wives; they only depend, as I said many times, on this reversible circularity between the metaphysical plane and the societal plane.

In logic, this system excludes, for instance, cohabitation and marriage with two sisters because it disrupts the circularity; it excludes debauchery and prostitution because they constitute a useless excess: women are exchangeable in marriage and must be paid a "salary" (states the Quran): why and what is the point of debauchery, for God's sake! The system abolishes sodomy and sapphism because it is a perversion, a reversal of the system of circularity; it is the self-devastation and self-destruction of the genealogy and the lineage; it abolishes marriage between a Muslim and a non-Muslim because this misalliance breaks the circle, introducing other laws of exchange, other metaphysical principles and quite simply a chaos, an anarchy in the logic of the system.

For such a system to function, it must be absolute and closed in on itself; it must be regulated by immutable laws, inscribed definitively in the Quran—the figure of the circle turning on itself endlessly and according to the figure of double death and double life.

One can therefore speculate as much as one wants on the morality of this system, but our logical proposition can be verified from beginning to end, in all the provisions pertaining to marriage: repudiation, remarriage, inheritance, lawful and unlawful women. It is this rigor (in every sense of the word) of the system that could properly designate the closure of the Islamic system and the position of women in this system, including in heaven. Women in heaven? They are, as we all know, purified and chaste women, beautiful *houris* with big eyes, like rubies and coral. From the chastity recommended on earth to the virginity of the *houris,* sexuality is eternally circular. We come back to Adam and Eve's lost paradise: the circle is closed. This is (Islamic) eternity—and its vertigo.

(1982)

5

Bilingualism and Literature

We begin with a bad joke: It took us Maghrebis fourteen centuries to learn the Arabic language (more or less), more than a century to learn French (more or less), and since time immemorial we have not been able to write Berber.

This is to say that bilingualism and plurilingualism, in these regions, are not recent facts. The linguistic landscape of the Maghreb is still plurilingual: diglossia (between Arabic and its dialects), Berber, French, and Spanish in the north and south of Morocco.

In spite of this importance, bilingualism and plurilingualism are rarely analyzed. And obviously it is not in a few pages that the issue can be advanced. Here I have limited myself to a reading exercise based on a literary work written in French. And I have recently had the opportunity to point out the importance of this task for Maghrebi literature of French expression: "As long as the theory of translation, of bi-language and pluri-language has not advanced, certain Maghrebi texts will remain impregnable through a formal and functional approach. The 'mother' tongue is at work in the foreign language. From one to the other takes place a constant translation and a conversation *en abyme*, extremely difficult to bring to light ... Where does the violence of the text emerge, if not in this chiasmus, this intersection that is in fact irreconcilable? Again it must be noted, in the text itself: to assume the French language, yes, in order to bring to light this fracture and this *jouissance* of the foreigner who must constantly work on the margins, that is, only for himself, in solitude."[1]

Talismano is the name of Abdelwahab Meddeb's novel.[2]

To begin with, I shall not open the book straight away. I shall pretend to leave it folded on itself, standing there like a stele.

I shall first question the title, the first and last names that make a sign—to what, to whom?

Tremendous importance of the name, already questioned by several approaches, but I shall only consider here the literary effect of bilingualism and the process of translation, which emerge thus, from the start, as a double introduction to the text that is yet closed and waiting to be deciphered.

There is always an anguished joy in opening a book—a feeling of uneasiness that reminds me of that of writing—fear and apprehension of what unnameable?

Before these leaves open, *it has already begun*. Beginning of the book: beginning without beginning, time of writing, for which the book—open or not—is only a crossing, a kind of pause marked, demarcated, and driven by writing that works on its behalf.

The author, the reader as well, is faced with the following: to dare to begin where the beginning has taken place in an elsewhere endlessly receding toward the unprecedented, where the erasure of the subject is played out in every way.

You can wrap the text, add a notice, and elaborate the presentation and the title, but it has already begun.

How can the author (followed by his commentators) find, or rather place, himself in the beginning without beginning?

Yet as soon as the first word is put down, the whole scene of writing is already there. In every act of writing, a distinction should be made between the one dictating, the one writing, the first reader (of one's text), and the reader (of any other text). Dictation in the musical sense is an exercise that "consists," says le Robert, "in writing down musical phrases as one hears them." A certain homology between music and writing—it is the scansion, the rhythm of the body that speaks and dictates itself. That the dictation should be heard in the voice of a god, a master, or any other law does not uproot the question of the body from its space inhabited by words. Language writes us and reads us. The scansion of the body is the spacing of what is called scription. The "subject" who writes is not the one who writes, but the one who hears himself, writes himself, and reads himself in the same act.

It is step by step that the writer will win and lose everything at once, including his text and his proper name; it is step by step that the book that will come about designates itself at its closure, at its stele—process that cannot go back to its beginning.

I would like to talk of this beginning very slowly, without dealing now with the structure, themes, and forms of this or that statement; or if I were to deal with them, it would be, it would have to be in the future perfect.

Again about this beginning, I shall say (and this is no discovery of mine, but a discovery of language and its classifications) that *Talismano* (the title of the book, the cover of the book) opens with the phoneme "A," which initiates the author's first name: a dull and insignificant fact, by all appearances. But in this first letter, already a translation, or rather a complete transformation is at work. "A" replaces the (ع), phoneme not known to French and which, according to an archaic pictography (called Hamito-Semitic), is the sign of the eye: it began with an absent eye, with blindness, the invisible and the illegible.

Theoretically, this illegible is all the greater since Western linguistics has reduced Arabic writing to an alphabetical order, which is to say, a so-called consonantal-vocalic structure.

But as Moncef Chelli reminds us, classical Arabic grammar itself uses other concepts such as *al-sawamit* (the silent, the mute) for consonants and *al-harakat* (movements) for vowels and diacritical points. This linguistic thought of movement, stasis, and silence, which belongs to another logic, to another metaphysics of the sign, demands to be addressed in its element of theorization and classification.

Ethnocentrist reduction cannot identify the relationships between monolingualism, bilingualism, and plurilingualism. This statement has significant implications when one thinks of Arabic calligraphy, for instance, which transforms, when reading, the very utterance of a text—or when one refers to the Islamic mysticism of letters.

I mention this entire problematic only to show the difference that is inscribed, bilingually, in this "A" and which is our main concern for the moment—and thus, to bring to light a certain unthought of this transformation that means that from the very first letter of the cover, from the very first letter of the first name (of the author), nothing comes back to the mother tongue, or to the other for that matter.

To write in French for a foreigner (Arab) is this paradox.

It is tempting to present this transformation quickly according to an "Oedipal" figure. And it is one, inevitably. A figure that comes to mind from one phoneme to another, from one first name to its translation: in this "A," the author pronounces that which he does not read; he says that which he does not see, or more precisely, he pronounces to himself that which he does not read, he says to himself that which he does not see. Irreducible chiasmus.

The comment is not really unfair. But before we continue down this path, in this pattern of (first) naming and of the author's proper name, I would now like to open the book according to a fold, a single one, which runs through almost every page. It is a kind of hallucinatory phrasal attack and devouring incantation; it is the excessive use of the preposition "à" and it is not by chance—as for the generation of the text, in every sense of the word "generate"—as if the grave accent compensated for the transformation of the (ع); as if, from one language to the other, a phenomenal substitution devoured and haunted the text while keeping alive the bilingual dream that Maurice Blanchot talks about.

As if, such is the bilingual text, on the margins of the untranslatable. Further below, it is in this direction that I shall go through the text.

At the moment I open the text anywhere. I did it, do not believe me if you do not feel like it. I read page 148 [T.N. of the French edition], and I highlight only the "à"[3] which marks a verb.

[A] Leave these shores of Eden after swimming, [à] walk despite the scorching heat, gravelly streets of the town practically deserted, lament of bare feet that must choose between sharp stone and melting tar. [A]

Walk by the Prefect's residence, [à] leave behind the school for girls, [à] knock at the locked door of the Cultural Center, [à] finally come upon the only street with any life at this hour, stalls open, siesta pursued at counters, dozing merchant drooling in slumber, flies swarm, scattered patrons dozing in coffee shops, scented souks of the city, colors bright even in shade, scarves, bolts of cloth, indifferent sides of beef. [A] Enter a sleepily seedy café: here reigned lethargy, a couple of indolent elders secreting a lofty presence. [A] Ask for a hookah, honey-soaked maasal tobacco, būrī, masrī, the national brand distinct for its 'agami tombac, plant of Persia or Mesopotamia. [A] Smoke headless in this scorched land of Egypt. Reassuring to be acephalous fauna. To edifying puffs were added sips of thick black tea; [à] thirst suppressant.

   Café proprietor, an old Nubian, octogenarian perhaps, white tunic, stooped shoulders, chest hair gray, eyes small and wet, sparse beard, coarse fingers, nails blackened and broken. [A] Gets up, [à] comes over, [à] asks: where are you from? [A] My reply: from the land where the Banī Hilāl emigrated. (139–140)

Succession of attacks, a-ttacks in the beginning, in the middle, and throughout the text hallucinated by this letter and its transformation.

For the moment, I am trying not to refer the text to a particular form and style of French (or other) literature in which it could be grasped and reduced. I am first marking a trait, a blank, a difference in bilingual situation in relation to the author's first name, whose second letter (b) is common to both French and Arabic according to the usual classification of the two "alphabets."

This transformation of the first name is enacted by the author himself, either through the insistent call to the Muslim mystics' alchemy of letters, or by analyzing directly his signature. Let us open the book:

present at my birth, he (the grandfather) is said to have paraphrased Ibn 'Arabī: *It is a gift as Seth is a gift for Adam ... the son is the secret reality of his progenitor ... Every gift in the entire universe manifests itself according to this law ... no one shall receive anything that does not issue from himself.* And I still carry that native utterance in my body, for it was to be the origin of my name: Am I not persistently called the servant of He who gives? To find I am sealed by my name into the act of giving, here is what leads to excess in debauchery, to squandering of fortune! (158)

Servant of He who gives, of Allah the Giver—this is what reconstitutes, through a translation, the author's inaugural signature. We can therefore say that the first name would be given by the grandfather's reminder, as gift to the Giver, gift to an invisible god who names, gives, and disseminates the first names thus borne among his ninety-nine attributes, but removing from them the *al*, the article of his unique and absolute attribution. Rosary of first names according to the genealogy of a gift that *returns* to its Giver, in other words, for us, *a gift that is not a gift*.

How to subvert one's first name? To bear such a first name, such an attribute, requires losing it in language (the language of the other), erasing oneself in language in writing, not only between Allah and the language of the Quran, but also confronting it from without through a foreign language.

Thus, the bilingual text—whether it likes it or not—tracks the exile of the name and of its transformation. It falls under a double genealogy and a double signature, which are just as much the literary effects of a lost gift, of a giving that is severed in its origin. A double gift, what is it? The foreign language gives with one hand and takes with the other.

For the foreign language, as soon as it is interiorized as actual writing, as words in act, transforms the first language, structuring it and driving it toward the untranslatable. This is what I shall put forward— the so-called foreign language does not add itself to the other, nor does it enter a relation of pure juxtaposition with it—each *signals* to the other, summons the other to maintain itself as outside. Outside against outside, this strangeness—what a language desires (if I may say so) is to be singular, irreducible, and rigorously other. I think (and I shall come back to this very important point) that translation operates according to this intractability, this endlessly receding and disruptive distancing. And as a matter of fact, all this Maghrebi literature of French expression as they call it is a narrative of translation. I am not saying that it is only translation; I am pointing out that it is a narrative that *speaks in tongues.*

Reconstitution of the name, after that of the first name. Let us first follow the novel:

> The name spells me: of the first name, servitude expressed already as gift, nothing further to add there; not that you're tight-fisted or an outrageous spendthrift (. . .).
>
> The family name, however, is another matter: originally Mu'addib, schoolmaster, teacher, prescriber of knowledge for its proper usage in society, dispenser of adab, a purveyor by name of good breeding and official culture, for the training of scribes and other executives of Arab power.
>
> But language slips in usage from ritual purity toward demythologized dialect, the genealogical real: thus, Mu'addib changes into Middib; a phonetic fate that's not at all trivial, because the meaning shifts—the task of education becoming that of nursery-school teacher: the middib is the one who, with the Koran as excuse, teaches children to read and write.
>
> (. . .) The French transcription of your name, stigmata of colonial intervention, claims to lighten its load with a new spelling, municipal duty, respecting neither the phonetic resemblance nor the logic of transliteration, Middib becomes Meddeb, quirky habit of altering spelling and sound ascribed to some Corsican civil servant, some Alsatian brigadier. (207–208)

Transformation of a name: from the sacral and literary *koiné* to the Tunisian Arabic dialect (diglossia), then from diglossia to the French (colonial) script: the Arab author of French language is the literary effect of this double transformation, this perturbation.

I will not follow the genealogical order described by the author. I shall focus my attention not on this reconstitution, this *a posteriori* of the name, but rather on the concrete situation, even if it means subsequently identifying its ramifications in this *koiné*. The situation is the following: the dialect is inaugural in the body of the child; the written language is learned afterward, and in the colonial period, this

Arabic language and writing were fought against, suppressed, and replaced in the service of the French language. Such is the archeology of the child.

Which means that the genealogical primacy of naming for the individual who will write in French is not, in the singularity of its narrative, that which is derived from the Quran and from the written language, but that the diglossia between the spoken and the written, between the inaugural maternal speech and the language of the (Islamic) law, the Name of the Father and writing, that such a scission will be populated, cut, hallucinated, played out in a third code—French—and that the whole edifice of language will be modified according to this substitution.

We cannot say that this is a strictly bilingual situation according to standard usage, or that it is a situation of three absolutely heterogeneous languages, but rather of a third code that *initiates* a diglossia and transforms the whole of what is said and written.

This is an eminently complex situation, for as third language, French substitutes for the diglossia by *translating itself from the French into French*. Nodal point on which I shall comment further below, and which means that the bilingualism internal to all language (from the communicable to the incommunicable, from "prose" to poetry) brings about a separation, an act of scission, of difference and transmutation, according to a movement that constantly doubles and splits itself. And the literary text (every text) would be the scenography of this forked enunciation. The French language is not the French language—it is more or less all the inside and outside languages that make it up and undo it.

In order to be done with the cover page, let us note that the title of the book—*Talismano*—is in Italian, and the word comes from the Arabic *tilasm* and from the Greek *telesma*. This designation is not by chance. As a matter of fact, the text is peppered throughout with Italian words. Here, Italian is the language of pure *jouissance*, heavenly language and language of the hedonic game, away from the violent contradiction of French and Arabic. Whether he uses Italian words and expressions or describes Italian cities, arts, and landscapes, the author is immersed in joy. Read with me, for instance, this passage on Venice:

> Venice, all glittering gold! How to capture the strained, sporadic, tentative, painstaking flight of your seagulls? And the Giudecca extends before eyes ravished by contemplation of lightly rippling watery space, undulating surface caressed by the wind. The cityscape extends to the outer shore beyond the church of the Salute: time won't allow me to venture into that uniform horizon that culminates in near ruin, factory yards, proposing yet another abandoned architecture that finally emerges as monumental, thanks to all the timid imitations: so what could that white Palladian façade be, so Redentore-like while making majestic use of a double-order façade not unlike that of San Giorgio Maggiore where one spends countless hours of contemplation and dissolution without ever quite exhausting the seething strands of light that pulsate within its irrevocable limits, blurring thought and reducing capacity for analysis to a steady nothingness. (26)

Italian, here, language of absolute *jouissance*, noncontradictory and utopian. It is this language that gives the title, and it must be noted that the only French words, or rather names inscribed on the cover, refer to the name and designation of the publisher. And already on the cover we are in this previously announced process of translation. I recapitulate this story of the first glance cast upon such a cover: what appear to the reader are therefore a first name and a name that are foreign to the language of the book. And below—a likewise foreign title, but it is less so in relation to French. Therein is a decrescendo of difference, a differential *jouissance* that is closer and more familiar.

But where does the *jouissance* of textual plurilingualism (cf. Joyce, Segalen, Pound) lie? As soon as bilingualism and plurilingualism are haunted by an untranslatable outside, authors resort to fragments of other languages, as if the text were not supposed to return to its own language and were multiplied into an always more deferred *jouissance* and an elsewhere that leads the unsayable, the silence, the madness of writing, and the confusion of languages to withdraw into their limits.

To speak in tongues is the narrative of this madness under surveillance. But the situation can turn around, sweeping the author away, shattering him in acts of madness and unreason.

The story of the great plurilingual text (Joyce) provides laws of narration internal to the act of such a (mad) *jouissance*. And it is not by multiplying words and fragments of different languages from here and there that the text thus justifies itself and can bear (itself) its abysses, its deviations, its telescoped dreams, its translations and confusions between one language and another, but it is indeed written by an almost imperceptible thought that turns and crosses into the unthought—the silence, the untranslatable, the always-there of the unnamed. Such laws, which develop according to the syntax of the body, cannot be "plated" onto the surface of the text—for they are the narrative of languages that speak on their own account, the narrative of the voice that is no longer infinitely separated from writing. Breath that lets me say irresistibly— Talismano, and not, for instance, talisman or tilasm or telesma.

Of course, the author makes explicit his intentions and even amuses himself by reproducing (on p. 133 of the original French edition) a talisman reconstituted according to the requirement of the text, a talisman made up of Arabic words and sayings, of emblematic drawings and a Chinese ideogram (*The Way of Tao*). He also amuses himself by translating this talisman while commenting on it and describes how, in his work, this talisman brings together Islamic mysticism (of the ipseity of *Huwa*: He, Allah) and Taoism, and makes them meet (p. 143 of the English edition). From the Italian language to the Chinese—the *jouissance* of the elsewhere, of the impregnable. This is the process of a certain substitution of bilingual suffering—to deport the contradictions, clashes, encroachment of identities and differences complicated by the dual game of bilingualism. Swerve toward utopia, that is, a place of writing that is not unreal, but the place of the hedonic impossible.

The author amuses himself and makes explanations, commenting on himself from page to page, having to gain step by step (gain and lose) what he desires to see in his singular experience, and what passes through it, which is again to say the double transformation from written language to the dialect and from diglossia to the French language, in this text.

Let us take a closer look. We shall follow the author's words, but reversing the reading order he proposes. Why? Because the genealogy of his languages is a reconstitution. I shall rather begin from the site of dialectical speech. Why this reversal? The so-called mother tongue is physically inaugural; it introduces to the saying of the non-said of the confusion with the mother's body, and thereby to what cannot be erased in any other learned language, even if this inaugural speech falls apart and crumbles. The fact will remain that in its substitution maternal speech is irreducible to all radical translation. Its uprooting itself makes it work in *disruption*. In the end (of my account, here), maternal speech, precisely because it is not written and not elevated to the concept of text, harbors the memory of a narrative, and its genealogical primacy, even if reversed and deported toward an absolutely different language, will also say: it has already begun.

Then how does this maternal speech work in *Talismano*?

Before attempting to answer in terms of textual practice, it should be pointed out that among the many paths of analysis, I shall choose two:

- First, this place that I shall call workshop as proposed by the novel, which often explains its intentions (commentary on the book by the book, as it writes itself);
- Then, I shall bring up the question of what is no longer based on the author's intention, on his will, to keep the text under the sway of his haunting obsessions and within the limits of a certain theorizing speculation.

These two approaches are necessarily drifting, coming together or drawing apart according to the suffering economy of such bilingualism. I only unite or separate myself through such attention given to suffering, and not only for a principle of method.

And here psychoanalysis is inevitable—concerning what is called the "language of the unconscious." But as I am not operating on the basis of an analytical discourse while at the same time making use of a conceptualization that resorts to it; it is necessary, each time, to indicate its modalities of use in relation to the bilingual situation. For, in turn, bilingualism (or plurilingualism) poses immense questions to all discourse that claims to be Freudian, and since psychoanalysis (here I am referring to the French or francophone reader who only reads Freud translated into French) is a particular translation, it is perfectly and rigorously legitimate and urgent to compare psychoanalysis with the languages that work and translate it; and since all discourse is caught in a dense set of codes that are irreducible to a literal translation, it then happens that the whole question of the sign, signifier, signified, and signification is implicated in a metaphysics, science, and art of saying whose frameworks remain open to any interrogation.

I proceed here on the basis of a language (the one I am writing and speaking right here) in bilingual position, which can put itself into play and into crisis only if it is placed in a sufficiently precise topography that is movable from one language to another and capable of following the process of translation that takes place in the totality of the corpus chosen here, that of a novel.

This is an enormous task. I am delineating—in an ad hoc fashion—nodes, sutures, and ruptures from one language to another, where arise permutations and perturbations, where *jouissance* goes mad, suffers, eroticizes itself from one language to another, the one plus the other *and* the one minus the other, monumental substitution punctuated by the syntax of the body in its position of dictating, writing, and reading.

The first point—the workshop, as it is enunciated and announced. I first chose maternal speech, not only for the genealogical history of the one who writes and signs instead of the mother and after her by projecting himself toward the outside (the French language) that brings about, generates the text in the perpetual murder of the mother—not only by reason of this second rupture of the umbilical cord (linguistically) that Kateb Yacine talks about, and of this inner exile, drawn from the obstetric pain of the child destined for bilingualism, but also for a theoretical reason, that of *simulacrum*—splitting, breaking of the monolanguage and its swerve, its movement of transference from one language to another (and in every sense of "transfer"). Splitting, which puts itself on stage, and which cannot return to the Name of the Mother, the latter constantly named and unnamed by the foreign language, which transforms the last and first name of the author. Therefore a game of simulacrum, where "the origin" (the dialect, the dia-lect) seeks to speak, to emerge in the text through an erasure in suffering and, managing to return to itself, falls apart.

This is a question of the madness of writing through several languages, in a genealogical diagraphy. Madness and the becoming mad of writing thus: I shall move further along this path.

Having said that, I shall now focus on the workshop.

Let us cite a few very simple examples of the lexical use of the Arabic dialect:

1. "I find I'm feeling fully medina-minded, *medinating.*" (19)
2. "an ancestral *sebsi,* bone and metal stem with clay bowl, to be filled with kif." (23)
3. "*guiddid,* meat dried and salted, leftover from sacrificial lamb." (79)
4. "cleansing waters from the sacred well, *zemzem,* rebirth and purification to resume life's blank page, reunion with his *fitra,* his innate temperament, blank slate." (83)

Rarely does the author put forward a word of the Maghrebi dialect without explaining it. He feels compelled to translate his vocabulary, to make a comment and sometimes coin these pidgined words: *médiner, en-khol-er* (in another context). In the fourth example, he explains both a dialectal word and a word (a concept) of the written Arabic by adding two words of commentary: *blank page.* From one to the other, a sacral purification and a theological closure; and to break the circle, let us remind ourselves that *fitra* derives from the verb *fatara*—to invent, begin, inaugurate, without any metaphysical connotation. What comes to disrupt this theological circle is the *blank page appropriated by a foreign language.*

But let us quote the whole paragraph that brings us to the Jewish alchemist Yaʿqūb:

> We leave the idol, this anthromorphic reconstitution of myth, right on the flagstones in her cylinder. We exit via the door that opens onto the wool souk, in search of Yaʿqūb. Most of the shops are closed, the covered souks mostly deserted. No sign of people shopping for carpets, hours and days of labor, sweat, desiccated lungs, twisted fingers, offering cheap exoticism to some, decryption of Providence to others, via this plush pilgrimage, return of the master pilgrim enthroned in his shop, gum arabic to sweeten the mouth, cleansing waters from the sacred well, zemzem, rebirth and purification to resume life's blank page, reunion with his fitra, his innate temperament, blank slate that awaits only the reed qalam and ink of days for the feverish birthing of an inaugural calligraphy, ivory bartered in the Sudan, ancient electric amber, coral from ear-splitting depths, rare pearl and wondrous shell, flora and fauna deep within sand, chest exploded, lungs burst, nostrils destroyed. (83)

I shall comment here on the whole. The alchemy of the text, its kabbalah between the (physical) correspondences of the thing and the sign—the writing describes the bric-a-brac of this alchemical melting pot that is Medina, that is this initiation that shows things by hiding the internal and archeological laws, and whose time, path of wandering (to medinate, to medinate!) reflects the topography of the text, its movement of jumping from one place to another, from one reference to another, from one language to another.

The author recalls his childhood. One enters it as one enters a dream, a dream fragmented in its initial saying, *a dream written by a foreign language.* A memory can only be translated. And this splitting of the dream constitutes the imaginary of this form of writing, radically divided between phonia and graphia, between diglossia and the French language, between irreducible alterity and the impossible return to the Same. No circle closes in on the identity claimed by the author.

Here is a power of amnesia *en abyme*, the substitution of one memory for another, or rather and more precisely—an embedding constantly broken, recovered, detached from its unity, movement caught in a vertiginous forgetting, which works to fragment itself endlessly. The theoretical question is the following: if one writes in French while the first language remains spoken, what becomes of the body of the dreamer when he is sleeping or writing?

Vast question. I shall suggest a global interpretation, for which I shall have to provide an explanation elsewhere. Then I shall say that the sleep of this first language, inaugural in the body of the child, introduces the aphonia, and sometimes the aphasia of the *night reciting in tongues*, and that what makes a break in a text and grafts itself onto it falls under the sway of the monolanguage—in this case other. The other, which becomes language minus all the others, the other that does not return to the same, the other, always the other. The untranslatable is not this unsayable, inaudible, and forever closed-off beyond, but a work of sleep and insomnia then, hallucinating all translation, dreaming for itself from language to language, and whose bits and pieces spring up day or night in the waking dream of all writing.

That is why this form of text is more or less hermetic—it seeks, in the linguistic confusion, an impossible clarity, *a clarity that suffers* in the text, a clarity of thought touched by the unthought. Such is this mad dream, beyond every Tower of Babel. The mad dream, whose exemplary experience was incarnated by Hölderlin.

The hermeticism of *Talismano*, whose explicit and explanatory side (the redundancy, the bombast, the overload) folds the text under a baroque shock. I call *baroque*—in a traditional and globalizing manner—the development of the *rhetoric* in relation to the *structure*. This baroque is not decided by the author, but by the edifice, the architecture of language that proliferates in telescoped patterns, sentences, and emblems in juxtaposition and interlocking together according to a disruption of the monolingual structure. The edifice of language carves out the fragmented body of the writer, stele, proper name, signature, grave, book beginning in the language of the other.

As to the question of death, I shall try to show below the duplicity that makes the text oscillate between God and its negation by the letter

of the other, God and its annihilation in a call for the Sufi trance. If
for the Biblical and Evangelical believer God created the languages and
separated them, which is to say that he *speaks in tongues*, all of them
and separately; and if Allah is moreover and for his followers the one
who privileges the Arabic language among all of them, the very one that
is historically known as the language of the *Quraysh* ethnic group (that
of the prophet Muhammad), what happens to the writer who adopts
and who is adopted by a "barbarian" language—as the Quran says? And
if it is a more or less subversive perjury, how does the consciousness of
his misfortune, of his separation with his God, graft itself onto his text?
What happens to his name in an enunciation that shatters the notion
of the One and the oneness of the divine voice? How to love—between
one's dead god, the mother tongue thrown to pieces and the barbarian
language?

Questions that will be taken laterally, following the path of the
text. Bilingual path going through crossings, detours, clearings from
language to language. When he comes to the end of his journey, the
author turns around, at the end of the book, in the last page of the book,
and says an illuminated prayer to what he calls "woman":

> (…) body, pleasure,[4] death, desert: all unutterable and transformed
> into moments of uttering by way of the language of metaphor, rendered
> archaic even to oneself, old as the world, to repeat that the light to
> brighten our lands shall come from women: by the planet Jupiter,
> by chrysolite, by Venus, by hematite, the female will make fertile the
> beds tread upon by male readiness; and by this new suffusion may the
> divided body recover its orphaned other. (262)

I let these references intersect without for the time being dealing with
their theoretical development, or with the necessity of a linear logic of
demonstration. The commentary turns with the text, each for its own
account.

An account that goes toward the incalculable. I have taken very
simple examples of use of the dialectal Arabic vocabulary, and this
selection proves infinitely complex to interpret. For the use of a word,

a single word (*zemzem*, for instance) carries with it the whole immense maternal corpus, which works silently and imperceptibly, and clumps together here and there in the book, as if, as Maurice Blanchot reminds us in his reflections on translation, the language to be translated could fold back on itself at any time, and escape the one who tries to appropriate it by a transmutation on a different ground, to divert it from its site by cutting it out of its context, leaving it as "dead language," as when one talks of mortmain property. Kateb Yacine states this very clearly:

> Never, not even in those days of success in the eyes of the (French) schoolteacher, have I ceased to feel deep within me that second rupture of the umbilical cord, that internal exile that no longer brought together the schoolboy and his mother except to wrest them, each time a bit more, away from the murmur of blood, from the reproaching shivers of a banished language, secretly in an agreement as quickly shattered as concluded ... Thus I had lost at once my mother and her language, the only inalienable treasures—and yet alienated, the only inalienable and yet alienated treasures![5]

But the mother tongue, which has begun, cannot disappear from the syntax of the body. Its disappearance would be a completely impossible hypothesis. Repressed, given over to silence and to the chasm of memory, this speech comes flowing back, scattering itself all over the texture of the book (*Talismano*).

It forgets itself, without forgetting itself, playing with the author: history of amnesia. Amnesia, yes, which pushes him to spell out once more that which endures, that which unravels in the foreign language. Yes, amnesia—a history of palimpsest, of that which works in a way beneath the white page, the erasure that springs from its trace.

The author spells—this is this, that is that. In these comments and explanations, already a translation, or rather the transformation of a *redundancy*, not in the usual pejorative sense of the word, but in its multiple meaning: overintense state of mind, excess, loss, repetition, amplification, superfluity, bombast, excess of rhetoric ornaments—a whole economy of overbidding which, apparently, says too much, which is to say, not enough. In bilingualism, this "too much" is by contrast the nerve of an always-late translation in relation to its processes. I would go so far as to say that what is at stake here is the mode of thought itself and its possibilities. Not thought in general, such as can be systematized, but a progressive-regressive thought, which unfolds from language to language. A dialectic indeed, but broken and unleashed—the violence of going mad[6] in the language of the other, of loving them by un-loving them—palimpsest of the splitting and the split.

If, therefore, in every text that respects these inherent laws, thought is not separable from writing (when they are separated, both are neutralized relative to each other); if it takes refuge in the movement, the scansion of the spoken body, rhythmed by all the idioms of memory and amnesia; if this is how it develops, then I would say that the bilingual or plurilingual text no longer implies a single mode of thought that would be capable of bringing them together. Every language presents (itself) thought with several modes, directions and sites, and the attempt to keep this whole chain under the law of the One would be the thousand-year-old history of metaphysics, of which Islam represents here the theological and mystical reference par excellence.

Now in this narrative, which is transcribed between a diglossia and a dead language, what would thinking be according to this unifying direction (in the French language)? And, from our perspective, what would thinking be according to this incalculable—to make from three the one, *and* from the one, the median, the other, the interval of this palimpsest?

I suggested—and Kateb stated it very clearly—that the Arab writer of French language is caught in a chiasmus, a chiasmus between alienation and inalienation (in all dimensions of the two terms)—this author does not write his proper language, he transcribes his proper name transformed; he cannot possess anything (if ever one appropriates a language), he possesses neither his maternal speech that is not written nor the written Arabic language that is alienated and given to a substitution, nor this other learned language that signals him to disappropriate and erase himself therein. Insoluble suffering when the writer does not assume this instituted identity, in *a clarity of thought that lives on this chiasmus, this split.*

I continue on the side of the Arabic language. The redundancy I underlined is not the sole literary effect of this maternal dialect. Whether he has recourse to a proverbial word, to sayings, fixed syntagms, and pidgined expressions; whether he transcribes as such whole dialectal statements (e.g., on p. 162 of the original French edition, on p. 170 of the English edition) or amuses himself by parodying the narrative or the popular style of the harangue and the dialogue, he tries to bring about all these processes in the impetus of the text, to control their repetition and iteration in a *running translation.* "So these are the waters the text is navigating, unobvious as that may seem," he writes (56). And casually, it risks at any moment wavering on its foundations, sliding into a trembling, a self-eating, where every castrated language is dismembered according to the *jouissance* of a fragmented body.

Fragmented body of which the author says, for instance, "that obsession, nothing but the maternal nucleus itself dislocated by hate and denial" (13), and whose mutilation, haunting obsession of a lost unity and an uprooted and exiled origin, punctuates this devastated energy. *The syntax would be the punctuation of the fragmented body.*

As to this fragmented body, the author recalls his encounter with Arabic writing, through the recitation of the Quran: "I encountered the father through the practice of the text. I endured the rigors of adapting to his rough mnemonic" (108). On the basis of this mnemonic he reconstitutes exactly, and not necessarily where he thinks he does, the initiation to pure significance—precisely that of the incantation of the Quran without the reciter understanding its signification.

This scholastic method of recitation has a double effect: on the one hand, such a method, with its agonizing violence for the child, introduces him rigorously to the Name of the Father: "There is no God but Allah." Such a tautology of unity, indivisible, which neither begets nor is begotten, signs the pact, the oath, the *Shahada* before

God. On the other hand, the child thus enters the time of the law of the book and writing. He recites, he reproduces what he does not understand: writing lesson to initiate the child to the invisible image of Allah.

By means of mnemonics, Islamic theology introduces itself to a *blank and empty writing*. The text (*Talismano*) that is a certain speculation on the void will not have broken this closure (including Islamic mysticism and its notion of *fana*: annihilation) so long as it does not take seriously the theological propagation in the Arab imaginary.

Through the reproduction and iteration of the sacred text, theology introduces writing in the strong sense of the term; it introduces the time of the trace, vocalization, the breath and the syntax of the body, toward the call to the Other, the Absent, the Invisible. That this operation (that can be turned around) is made in the name of an invisible God does not obliterate the important question: to name God in the language and time of the written word, is it not an inaugural initiation to the unnamed and the unnameable?

Subversion against theology, the sacred book and the Name of God, in this case, cannot operate from without, especially when one bears an attribute of this God; yet, for me, one would have to proceed in this direction: to think, as one writes, the end of every book (sacred or not) by working against one's proper name and signature.

That is why, in relation to the letter and writing, calligraphy as well as Islamic mysticism as yet remain the theoretical summits of theology.

I have discussed elsewhere the issue of the art of calligraphy in Islam, and I do not wish to come back to the global questions it gives rise to—but rather, I continue to discuss in this book the use it makes of the Arabic language, and thus to put myself to the test, since I have always been very interested by the relation of the calligraphic line, and since this relation happens to be called for—and not by accident—by *Talismano*.

The author devotes lengthy passages to this relation—commenting on some moments of the mystical states, such as ecstatic writing—whose theological orientation he wants to divert. References abound, very often explicitly stated and sometimes implied: I mention here Al-Hallaj of *Kitab al-Tawasin*, the Persian Suhrawardi, and above all Ibn Arabi with his monumental encyclopedia *al-Futūhāt al-Makkiyya*, through which his mysticism, by means of a very singular Neoplatonic thought, grounds itself simultaneously on the Quran, cosmogony, and arithmetic, in order to build a science of letters in the cosmic hierarchy, which this exceptional mind has elaborated with such remarkable and also poignant writing. I also do not forget the sect of *Ikhwān as-Safā*.

These texts the author cites as he tries to incorporate them are marked by an extremely complex history of the link between the letter and mystical experience. I shall not advance my commentary on the totality of this experience. I would like to draw attention to what motions Arabic writing when language, which the linguists call a "target-language," is struck by a reversal with respect to the "source-language." These two notions are useful but of limited effectiveness; they refer to metaphysical designations of the sign, origin, copy, and translation. But then what happens in this book? What becomes of the trace of the Arabic letter when it appears in the text?

In the situation I described, Arabic writing splits itself as it translates itself into a Latin writing, which obeys a different graphemics and has not developed a particularly calligraphic art: this is not a lack, the Latin graph having taken elsewhere its scriptural line.

Therefore, the French writing that restructures the entire *Talismano*, marking and demarcating a game of palimpsest, thus reverses the relation of the "target language" to the "source language," or more precisely, the "source language" that is a diglossia between the phon and the graph becomes itself the "target language." Reversed letter, which calls for calligraphy in Islam, in this erasure of the Arabic letter that comes back without coming back, that appears without carrying along the text. And how could it? It would be a kind of madness to think that a language (no matter which) can write and rewrite another from within, and can tame it according to a perfectly invisible law. However, such a desire of *radical transposition*, of extraordinary crossing from one language to another, passes through certain texts tempted by the untranslatable.

Here the book happens to be torn by it, sometimes shattered into pieces. Something that belongs to the madness of speaking in tongues in a unified writing inhabits the imaginary of those who suffer from it in the reversal of the ordinary language-to-language relations: relations that specify for each its distinct property, its separate territory, and its resistance to all translation. The extraordinary would be to write in a way with many hands and many languages, in a text that is but a perpetual translation.

In this book, Arabic writing (its calligraphy) returns as commentary on itself and on its absence and repression, the redundancy of what cannot come to pass as absent text; elsewhere that is however the elsewhere of the source language, a lost source. From there, a whole rhetorical deployment on what the author calls the "void,"[7] in place of the "Name": Allah. To pierce, to burst the texture of the book through traces, perforations, divestments in the body fragmented between diglossia and Latin graphia—this is how this reversal is haunted.

And along this path, the author draws Islamic calligraphy toward mysticism (the mystic letter), and the latter toward the notion of the "void." Notion that remotely recalls the Tao, since Tao is accessible to the author through the French language. He brings face-to-face Chinese ideography and the calligraphy of Islam—the face-to-face of fascination, fascination of the extreme, the extremely remote, *jouissance* of the untranslatable.

Let us take another example. Henri Michaux, the Belgian, draws inspiration from Chinese ideograms in order to draw, and his drawings are neither Chinese nor Western. For the pleasure of the graph removed from its origin—other palimpsest.

But the word is not silent in the face of the untranslatable. On the contrary, the latter can enable thought, so much so that to think between several languages is a *mad thought*. It may be madness, it may be reason, but a mad thought works to shake metaphysics, insofar as the latter opposes reason to unreason, thought to unthought.

When the author calls upon fragments of elsewhere (Italy, China), he lends himself to this vertigo of fascination.

I said he draws Arabic calligraphy toward mysticism (the mystic letter) in Islam. Let us read these lines on the word (on p. 219 of the original French edition), or rather on the word *Hanīf*, sacred name (in Islam) of Abraham or Ibrahim, if you will:

> Hanīf, Abrahamic word, predating things Arab, rousing the pagan body. Of the letter *ha*, that of *hāl*, or state, fullness of the moment, heightening the flash of certainty, distancing you from the man of doctrine, of *maqāl*; of the letter *nūn*, emphatic graph extolling *nūr*, light to incorporate, to bequeath, to enlighten the self, not simply to confront its reference to the sun, think in terms of the Verse of Light and its commentary by Al-Ghāzali, *The Niche of Lights*, which has recovered its rightful place in the hierarchy of Enlightenment, by Mazdaist contribution, by Suhrawardian incandescence; of the letter *fā'*, to say *fā'l*, good omen, unique to each, for every person is in the world an irreplaceable herald, an idiosyncracy of sex, of being, of death, of text, of idiolect, the self observed, outside the convergence of interests (. . .)," etc. (208–209)

The objection is that how can a text be double while it keeps at a distance its laws of construction, its workshop, and all the texts that inhabit and haunt it?

Question of every text, obviously, but I mark here the game and scenography of the double and the palimpsest that can be played out, strategically, in a number of ways—either the text operates a continuous translation of what it says (this is that) or it takes place and conspires against its references (here, the Arabic language), erasing all explicit reference, and if reference there is, it takes place in the production of the text, not elusive, but in inhering disruption. This is what I call *translating from French into French*, in a silent passage from the foreign language into the latter. Textual bilingualism would be the movement of this rather strange palimpsest, in loss on itself, on its origins and genealogies. I would go so far as to say that such a text is double, because it is sustained, silently and in pure gratuity, by the mother tongue. It becomes translatable on the other side such that the target language works to silence and erase itself.

This is the beginning of reading this book in *French*. All I have done is initiate a protocol of reading and transposition from one language to the other.

Questions of Art

Flight of the roots

I met both of them.

I met Ahmed Cherkaoui in 1961. Together we would discuss national culture, the search for an art given over to its radical question, the question of taking root again and of pointing to a different path.

Cherkaoui died suddenly in August 1967, upon his return to Morocco.

In turn, Jilali Gharbaoui died in April 1971, one night, in Paris, on a park bench. Image of abandonment and weariness, familiar to his friends.

I have always imagined Gharbaoui as a stranger to our daily hustle and bustle. The way he spoke timidly, never completing a sentence, marked a queer distance, gently balanced in a detached drunkenness.

But a work of art cannot be circumvented by lived experience, even an overwhelming one. We know that lived experience in itself is empty. It is necessary to always introduce a question for it to be able to resonate with the vibrant intimacy of its being. Art speaks from the veins of its most veiled roots, and retires to the lived.

Veiled roots—let us for a moment focus on these two words. Moment that is first held by a recent memory from a trip to Malaysia. I thus evoke the image of a gigantic tree whose branches, apart from the trunk, abundantly come down to the ground, and with passion sink into it. The strength of the trunk persists but is noticed implicitly—apperception veiled by the branches that thus contribute to the being of the root and to the being of the branch.

In this movement, the root returns, deviated, to its own element. No doubt, the tree's destiny is to take root and stretch out to the sky, but here the tree takes hold and soars up in accordance with a double and circulatory impetus, as if the second movement of its impetus (branches veiling the trunk) freed the tree from the earth, and the earth from its depth. Thereby, the liana overflows the elements that sustain and nourish it. The blood of thought is a fiction of the tree.

The radical veil transports and suspends the earth according to a flight of the roots. This flight that is born in an intractable light accommodates the tree in a raised form—and not torn from its absolute stipe. It is therefore inexhaustible in its effects of transposition. But perhaps it is necessary to repeat with the usual risk that art, in its cardinal disposition, orients itself by flowing in the captive freshness of the source.

"He neither serves nor commands, but only acts as a go-between. His position is humble. He himself is not the beauty of the crown; it has merely passed through him,"[1] writes Paul Klee.

This image does not change the question of the tree, but it underscores a variation regarding the ever-unheard-of question of identity. I talked of Cherkaoui and Gharbaoui. I briefly mentioned the events that marked their death in order to imply their nominal connection. Where is the liana of such an evocation? First, in the literality of the word— al-Gharbaoui means Western, Cherkaoui Eastern. That alone: this is—in a way—the whole question of Arabic art between the East and the West.

The word *maghrib*—place where the sun sets, the west. By extension, extreme distancing. Always a horizon that calls the journey, the exile, the separation from the birthplace.

Painting celebrates in its own way the cardinality of a country; it celebrates the hidden color of the origin. In its geographical layout, Morocco is metaphorically a setting of the sun into the sea.

It is that the country is placed in a revolving site, and that thus embedded into the sea (to the north and west), Morocco leads to the desert from the south and east. Slipstream of elements, which awaken painting to an intoxication of the sun, to such an intense brightness that it shakes the hard support of objects. Yes, what is a native soil given over to the visible? What is a native soil?

Morocco was thus chanted by Europe, already by Homer, and circa 1300, by Dante—chanted like a distant land dreamed-of in the radiance of the myth. That of Ulysses, and it is not by chance—Ulysses is the first narrative of wandering.

Does not the name Barbary come from a similar representation as well? The name *maghrib al-aqsa* (far west) was given to Morocco by the Arab East. Let us not forget that *gharīb* (root *gharaba*) has a major double meaning—strange, stranger.

Sharaqa expresses the idea of the sunrise and its light; it also expresses, in an absolute sense, the idea of radiance, when, for instance, the beauty of the face becomes metaphor of the sun. The West and the East move toward each other, in an endless beginning. Art is the other name of this journey.

The play of roots of a language imposes formidable questions. Their outline should be determined by the following: where does the ray that glides in Cherkaoui's painting come from? Cherkaoui's painting is monogrammatic. "Monogram," according to le Robert, "is a figure composed of the initial letter or several letters (initial or not) of a name, combined into a single character. Ex.: monogram composed of the initials of a first and last name, etc." In a general sense, the monogram designates an initialing, an abridged signature, the form of a proper name. It therefore refers to a calligraphy of roots.

A painting is monogrammatic when it makes visible the drawing, the interlacing of its identity. Identity as calligraphy of roots—art awakens within the duration of this return.

But in this quest, what should be kept in sight—beyond technical competence—is that which harbors things and objects in the flight of the roots and the intoxication of the sun—that which spells the dance of the native soil in its desert and its exile without return. Driven thus, art signs in the transposed eye of the sun the tracing of a proper name; it crosses the East with the West like two swords transfigured by the subtlety of a tattoo.

We have to briefly explain these metaphors: identity does not give itself as a euphoric and synthetic revelation of being, but in every way, it supposes the quest for an inescapable destiny. We are talking of the calligraphy of roots and of the dance of the sun, insofar as the being of painting glorifies color in the fire of its radiance and in the blueprint of things according to their vibrant projection. The root deviates by itself in order to vibrate in the wind.

I have always associated Cherkaoui's painting with the color mauve. However, he inevitably used a wide color range on the path of his destiny. No matter how many times I have seen his paintings, it is the mauve that keeps coming up, like the absolute color of the home country.

Was it a dream?

Let us now look at the vision of the monogram in its technical aspect. The monogram condenses into a simplified figure—diamond, triangle, stylized object. Figure definable by geometry and measurable by science. From there, an ingenuous geometrism of certain painters, here or elsewhere.

The composition of the monogram is a base motif, which disposes itself—with the strength of the hand—for a variation of colors and lines. An apparently simple composition, closed in on itself. To grasp the spectacle of the monogram, it is necessary to determine the different components that take different paths. Leading where? It is better to talk—with Klee—of the "hesitant twilight shades around the middle."[2]

Let us take the *estampe-étude* (1966) monogram in a semicircle (Figure 6.1 shows another artwork by Cherkaoui from 1964, *Le Couronnement*, since *Estampe-étude* could not be found.). A central line symmetrically cuts the page into two halves. The stick on the right attracts the semicircle, while a delicate and graduated punctuation works the posed verticality. Thus, a shaky balance takes shape in accordance with a calligraphy of signs. But what we should reflect upon is how the norm of a composition reaches the word. "The word and the picture," says Klee, "are one and the same."[3] How to reflect otherwise upon painting?

For painting to speak, the work must signify with precision. Cherkaoui felt the limits of geometrism, which reduces painting to a

Figure 6.1 Cherkaoui: The Coronation (1964)

pseudo-scientific construction. Geometrism makes the products of art into simple tools of a technical world. A common temptation to let the world flow as it does.

So here is Cherkaoui faced with the overriding question of technology and science, by which I mean their effects on art. Moroccan or not, the painter must not believe that he can with impunity borrow from the West its technical universe without being affected, caught by the history of Western metaphysics. If we accept Heidegger's proposition, the destiny of metaphysics and that of the essence of technology are all one. Those who use Western technology thinking they are removing its "soul" themselves remain caught in theology. We hear Arab painters claiming to make use of Western technology for the sole purpose of better signifying their national identity. What does this mean? The frenzy of wanting to incorporate contemporary Western knowledge without some understanding of its foundations is from the outset a relentlessly derisory experience.

In his own way, Cherkaoui patiently seeks to see clearly on this issue. He leans on Moroccan popular culture—tattoos, games of tapestry, all of which are forms of so-called decorative or symbolic signs. He feels within himself an irrepressible emergence of roots. Cherkaoui relies on this culture, inasmuch as his procedure already resembles that of the craftsman. In the game of carpets or tiles for instance, the master craftsman invents his own major motif, his monogram that animates the general texture. But Cherkaoui's question draws other concerns. While the call of the native soil resounds, he opens his painting to the calligraphy of roots. Quest curtailed by a premature death, but the calligraphy of roots has been at work always; it is an auroral inscription of art. The West and the East are, on the native soil, the shimmering of solar intoxication.

Calligraphy of roots. Where does this style of painting lie? In its social context, the tattoo stems from the tribal symbolic order—rites, healing, war markings. This is only of secondary interest to the painter. What circulates in the trace of the tattoo is the subtle being of desire. Cherkaoui commits his research to capturing the vibrations of the tattoo, what they say to the body. And by this gesture that is so difficult to maintain rigorously, Cherkaoui makes the tattoo and its own writing nonstrangers to one another. Slight and gentle metamorphosis. Velvety opening to the intoxication of the sun. Escape of the roots into the song of the tree.

Cherkaoui is, as they say, an abstract painter. He makes no concessions, neither to descriptive realism nor to sensualist pictorial Orientalism. Cherkaoui knew that painting is a writing of the sign. Yet, it should be noted that painting is such only so long as it suggests a cardinal disposition of being, retaining among its figures the world of nature, gods, and men—in the framework of its questioning.

Every theory of the visible is tied to the metaphysics of creation. That is why painting is always threatened in its foundation by a double vision—that of a representation of art, effect and reflection of the world (natural, divine, human), and that of a metaphysics of the void, according to which painting is this endeavor to wrest from the void an ensemble of signs, in order to give them back to it afterward in the form of their completion. That vision should be this wresting that would confer upon the world an incomparable plenitude is, it seems, the metaphysical principle of art. Have we come out of it?

The Maghreb enters European painting through Orientalist Romanticism. Event of election or mere transitory vision? What is, according to this Orientalism, the call of such an encounter?

Delacroix visits Morocco in 1832, Matisse in 1913, Nicolas de Staël in 1936. Klee, who, according to an ingenuous legend, is of Arab origin, exclaims in Tunisia in 1914, "I now abandon work. It penetrates so deeply and so gently into me, I feel it and it gives me confidence in myself without effort ... Color possesses me. I don't have to pursue it. It will possess me always, I know it. That is the meaning of this happy hour: Color and I are one. I am a painter."[4]

Happy hour! Exposed to the radiance of being, the East emerges in the form of things. The eye dilates, gives itself up to cardinal violence! The painter's song trembles in the absolute light. Happy hour of an encounter. In the heart of memory, we are enlightened by the question: What is then the East? The unforgettable East? The Unforgettable?

Let us undo the question in accordance with two visions (I am being much too schematic here, with all the risks it entails):

- the vision of a sensualist representation (in the French style), frustrated in its intimacy by an emotion of fear and *jouissance*. The sun does not appear as an errant illumination, moving the East and the West along the cardinal axis of being. The East would be a kind of exhilarating optical illusion.
- the scriptural vision (Klee), presenting the East in a hospitable word, celebrating the moving feast of the aurora and the crepuscular vanishing.

From one vision to the other, at stake is the metaphysics of representation; from one to the other, sensualism (in the French style) is left behind, although tailing it ever so slightly, we find it again in the Odalisques of Matisse.

Where to place in this Orientalism the flamboyant *élan* of Delacroix? Like all great works of art, that of Delacroix imposes on us its enigma. But it must be said what there is to say here and now, for Delacroix's equivocal vision leaves us perplexed.

How does Delacroix see Morocco? He sees it draped with the grandeur of the line, and mightily bristling in the rhythm of its violence. Morocco rears up in an absolute color.

Delacroix is torn by a very strong feeling of admiration and repulsion. In his letters from Morocco, he displays a somewhat ludicrous naiveté: he was surprised by the wariness of the Moroccans. Had he forgotten that he was accompanying an official political mission in a country that did not practice European-style painting? Here he is then, forced to paint often in secret, by memory. And not a single Muslim woman to pose for this very keen visitor who advised his Parisian friends, "Go to the Barbary States to learn patience and philosophy."[5] Delacroix discovers a light so strong that it makes vision alien to itself. The eye in exile in the intoxication of the sun—Delacroix's eyes ache, as he himself states. He also discovers, among the Moroccan people, a natural man, close to things and who at the same time reincarnates ancient Europe: "Rome is no longer in Rome," he writes. He also says, "The men of this noble race will move, for as long as I live, in my memory; it is among them that I have truly found the beauty of the ancients."[6]

But what matters for an artist is, above all, his work and not his ideology. Delacroix has celebrated the East with an intoxication of fire. Look at these agile horses, folded back on themselves. The earth takes off as the sky celebrates the luxuriance of its sun. Where to put one's foot in these soaring landscapes?

Likewise, the way in which Delacroix drapes horses and things— bold and proud gesture, bringing out the essential trait of a blazing passion. The drapery veils the body in a dancing beauty; it sets it in motion with the things of the earth and sky. Being lights up in its fold and the work of the artist attains the intoxication of the sun.

It was Klee's merit to have subtly defined the question of the East. The East here is no longer an unthought myth, a transient occasion of *jouissance*, but rather an emergence of roots through which identity is split in the effervescence of art.

The East is that site laid out in accordance with certain laws of hospitality and ferial generosity. And this East cannot be reduced to some ethnic or geographical origin; it welcomes the one who goes toward it as a guest who marches toward the rising sun. In this march, Klee is infinitely Oriental.

Klee thus saw the East as inner writing. And throughout its existence, the East obsesses him and surges back in his paintings. The stay in Tunisia was a historical event, but we are not naïve about Klee's ecstasy, in the quoted sentence. The East has always acted in us, but we do not know it enough.

In many of his works, and in particular for our purposes, in the *Arab Song* (1932) or *Oriental-Sweet* (1938), Klee carefully celebrates the meaning of this encounter. Every shade of color, every sign and symbol holds a free and amorous meditation: pulsation of a winged thought. The East is a tribute to the memory of the sun, a celebration of the Unforgettable.

That is why Cherkaoui is on Klee's side. That is how—for us—the meeting of Klee and Cherkaoui was necessary, beyond the pictorial sensualism and the metaphysics of representation. Cherkaoui died at the age of thirty-two, but the ray that illuminates his suspended work points at us the question of the calligraphy of roots.

And yet, the encounter can be problematic; it may mask a profound misunderstanding. Can a Muslim-born painter go toward the Face of Allah without already being enveloped by it? What does it mean to paint in an abstract manner an unfathomable Face? Where in this envelopment does the mystical Eros take shape?

Western painting has gone its own way, followed its own thought. "Own" is what ensures the constancy of the roots. No doubt, at happy moments, this painting encountered Eastern art, be it far or near. Again no doubt, nothing great and bright has remained untouched between the West and the East, nothing of what fulgurates in the dancing intoxication of the sun. Those of us who call for these happy moments, have we already forgotten the auroral lightning between Greece and Egypt? Have we forgotten the words of Plato, suggesting that barbarity is basically a retreat of the divine? What do we know of that which has always sheltered us in the faltering heart of Memory? What do we know of our hidden orientalness, constantly eluding our will to live? What do we know of our Face to partake in the burning of the sun? No abyss can miraculously divide the question of the origin in its exile. No historical misfortune. And if Destiny strikes us with fear, it is that the heart departs from its most irrigated thought.

The East is not dead, it has withdrawn; the West is not dead, it has gained power. Both refer to the truth of their highest promise. And we do not wish to lend innocence to the chorus of the Dull. Radical innocence opens to solar intoxication; it gives joy to those who march in the ensourcement of Destiny.

It took a whole thousand-year-old history for Western art to confront, in the beginning of the century, the experience of what is called the abstract. Not that there is a direct opposition between the abstract and the figurative (recent philosophy is undoing the oppositions inherent to the old metaphysics); not that from one style to the next, came about a revolution of the sun in the composition of colors and lines. But, as such and in its general feature, the abstract is another enchantment of the imaginary, through which painting, by becoming its own "subject," gives itself up to the specter of the pure sign. Blinding specter—just when he thinks he is innovating, the painter is caught in the grip of Technology.

In the figurative, the Face and the Thing are absolutes. The Thing tells of nature in its vibratile intimacy; the Face is not just the face in portraiture, it is the being of the body turned toward the divine. The Face is the vis-à-vis illuminated by heaven. And perhaps what they call abstract art has forever lost this angelic grace of Destiny. Abstract art has cut off the body from its Face, or at least the Face has erased itself in favor of a search for the pure sign freed from naturalist representation. Pure sign, in order to designate here the being of the absolute color, the absolute line.

Islam is a metaphysics of the Voice. It avoids the figurative and opens up to the sign as imprint of Allah. By (theological) definition, his Face is invisible. Art is immediately caught in the notion of divine creation. *Sawwara*, which gave *sūra* (image), means to represent, to give form, to create. *Tasāwīr* signifies idols, statues. Only Allah represents, gives form, creates. The artist, according to Islam, cannot claim to imitate the creative act of Allah, and wrest from the void a microscopic work.

More than a simple opposition to pre-Islamic totemism and to the Christian trinity (incomprehensible to the Muslims), this is a radical theory of the invisible, according to which the Quran is the integral text, the text of texts. It is in relation to writing that other forms of art signify and speak with one another. And if we have thus specified the calligraphy of roots, it is because it is inhabited by the Quran, inasmuch as it harbors the divine Voice. Language protects the roots and calligraphy celebrates their emergence. Calligraphy of roots, in all angles of the metaphor.

Islamic art avoids the figurative in its metaphysical ground. It avoids it without ever having eliminated it. And what it seeks in the vision of the world is the geometry of balance, the symbolic form of things, given over to the sacred. The metaphysical and historical path of art is necessarily different in every case. Klee arrives at the abstract through a long elaboration process of the figurative, and Cherkaoui through a return to the roots. Split and ambiguous movement, but the comparison brings to us the question of its range.

The journey leads Cherkaoui to a mystical nostalgia. The painter is possessed by Al-Hallaj's voice. And this is no chance nostalgia—the calligraphy of roots is governed by its reception of the sacred; it reaches for the beauty of the sun.

The mystic burns in the union of the beloved and the lover. He sees Allah and celebrates this gaze that goes through him. Transfixed gaze. Allah sees himself in the eye of the mystic.

Would Islamic-born painting be entirely enveloped by the betrothal to the divine? From where does it speak, now that it is the technology of the Dull that reigns? From where can it draw a new clarity? What is painting? What is Arab painting?

(1975)

Vertigo[7]

I would like to begin slowly, but very slowly, from a *rosace* mosaic without, for the moment, worrying about the questions that will follow as I go along, following a rotating and revolving movement of association, that movement which, drawing me to the rose, had, one day, put me outside myself—exaltation of the chiseled stone, by irradiating my eyes and my shaken body, demands still that I commit myself to this exaltation, this fascination, that I transcribe them in the place where my speech, still faltering and confused, is able to find its beginnings. As if, yes as if, intrigued and overwhelmed by the secret of a paradigm, I were called upon to initiate myself, by a constant and alert movement, to this rigorous symmetry of so-called forms and colors, a symmetry so strict indeed that it seems to burst out of the logic that holds it from within by moving toward that starred center of the mosaic, eight-branched center, orthogonal and orange point, which crystallizes the whole circular construction while keeping it liberated in its grace, turning in its rhythmic element—point where the void, in a way, rests, contemplates itself through the wonder that grows by taking hold: in every carved piece of the stone, every turn or junction of a perfect symmetry. Symmetry formed by hiding from the first spectator the cipher of its formulation.

I shall not describe the *rosace*. It describes itself—presents itself in all its pageantry. I rather want to say that what goes from the matter to the sign, and from the sign to my body taken by this *rosace*, demands at the same time the amorous translation of my agitation and a kind of artificial vertigo, essential to all infinite explication of art. Art would be this dazzled vacuity of time, the word intrinsic to art and to the effects of its exaltation—an offering between the unthought and thought.

Intrinsic word, by means of which art translates the unconscious, while the magic that enjoys it must watch over its thinking ordeal. Yes, this mosaic is a rhythm, going from the matter to the sign, and from the sign to language. Language, which, as it expands, unfolds, flows, and springs forth in these as yet unnamed decorative motifs.

Because of that, I uttered nothing about Islamic art in general— neither its overall forms and features nor its symbolic foundations, let alone a theory capable of framing and giving it the rigor of a resolute thought. I began from a long, a very long way off, from a detail—a *rosace*, and I am not even asking myself what is a *rosace*. For, to approach a work of art, thought is not enough, one needs the willingness of thought. But who can, without ingenuity, ensure that chance? Such a favor of consciousness? Besides, who would hope to initiate, and with their sole will, the outburst of such spiritual states, extraordinary states that must be transformed under the harsh law of the concepts, but concepts unfolding under the spell of a gift to knowledge? Can this knowledge, which is nothing but hard and irretrievable work, come to light in the bliss of saying without working against the passion that opens it out to an always-and-already-unknown transfiguration? I affirm this willingness of thought—in its most abstract sensuality— as cadenced alternation between the gravity of a splendid play (art and its celebrations) and this anguish, at times terrible and terrifying, which projects us toward the beloved work of art, in the forgetting of all will. Something extremely elusive is to keep us in front of the abyss. Position of being sustained only by the rift of an insisting thought. If I turn to this or that motif of art, to its creations, nothing can give me the certitude of thought about its chances. Therefore, it is essential not to rush, to maintain these moments of lightning and these tremblings in their initial sensation, alternation between gravity and fantasy, in accordance with the willingness of thought. I desire this joy, this upheaval, this grace.

Visibly, a mosaic is filled by all its splendors and the sumptuousness of its appearance. It appears, it has to appear—such is the work of enchantment the craftsman strives for as he fashions it, bears it within himself day after day, refined piece of his imaginary, carving, chiseling, coloring in his work according to his inspiration and his task. Vertigo of the void, which overturns in this mosaic. Lights, splendors. The void turns over and falls into the plenitude that is constantly warded off and concealed both at once. It is in this way, transfixed, that I see every wonder.

Now this gesture, which reveals the objects of art according to a syntax of enchantment, has long been a source of dreams, posing an enigma not only to the attention of any gaze, but also to every thinker, every artist tormented by the utterly peculiar idea of creation. This gesture has remained irreducible, and since the supposedly innocent and joyous infancy of art, the status of the latter has never ceased to intrigue the powers (of all orders) that are ardently tempted to seize and devote it to the glory of their image and their name, through and beyond death. This is of course glaringly blatant. Let us say this: we cannot elucidate in any respect the question of Islamic art if we do not keep in mind the inaugural message of the Quran, which is another question put to art as such. If then the Quran is considered as a divine text, whispered to Muhammad through the voice of the archangel Gabriel (I am not disputing this religious assertion, I am following firstly and briefly its itinerary), we should ask ourselves, before lending an ear to the extraordinary and the miraculous, what happens to the gesture of art in this revelation. Where to locate it in its blooming between gods, men, and nature? For, to begin from the theological, theo-philosophical, or mystical commentary of Islam is already to condemn oneself either to a hypostasis of the letter and the written sign (particularly in the example of calligraphy[8]) or to reproducing, in one way or another, the ideology of aniconism. In other words, the question of art would quickly be exhausted in that of religion, whereas it can only be incarnated in the body and the imaginary of the believer if it is a possibility to dream and be enchanted by the phantasmagorias of the invisible, according to this cyclical image referred to in the Quran—to die, to live, to die, to live everlastingly.

Now this Quranic passage of the double life and double death, ending with the eternity of the circle, raises innumerable questions on the being of nature, the thing and man, where these are transformed through the operation of art. But since the latter, such as we apprehend it, is an operation that gives back the visible to the visible by translating it, we would have to ask ourselves, who sees whom in this reversal of concepts (art and religion) between heaven and earth? What is envisaged by this conception of art dominated by the primacy of the Quranic text (writing, ultimately), and which calls the artist to celebrate an invisible world?

It is not just a god that is iconoclast and breaker of idols that Islam is faced with since its foundation in writing, but the truth of the invisible that constitutes every imaginary, religious or not. Truth, whose uncanny energy is constituted by—in this case monotheistic—belief and, stretched to its limits, has culminated in this dangerous and nonintermediated experience of the mystic, in these precisely unbelievable words: *Ana al-Haq'* (I am Truth: Allah), that is to say, I am the invisible itself. Cry of madness, as we have repeated, and it is so in ecstasy, but from this cry of Al-Hallaj's sprang secret poetic pages, in a remarkable mortification.

With these brief premises, we can already sense how Islamic art, in its intervention between God and men, is *unclassifiable*. Unclassifiable? Yes, considered as impossible imitation of a miraculous divine act (*i'jaz*) since only God is the creator; art is then subordinated to repetition, and as such does not possess any autonomy in principle—its function, subservient to an entirely religious mission: mosques, arabesques, illumination of manuscripts, calligraphy are all objects made for the glory of the invisible. By divine principle, there is no autonomy of art—or else God would be the artist par excellence, the creator of all images and all simulacra, which amounts to the same.

If then art, from our perspective, remains unclassifiable in this hierarchy of the visible and the invisible, Islam would be another name for this fundamental instability of the concept of art, if one accepts that the latter, which is not a concept in absolute terms, must detach itself from theology in order to tune up with thought and the willingness of thought, even if this means letting it come and go in its wandering indeterminacy, impregnable and unframable by any aesthetics. *Aslama* means to surrender, to make peace with one's Adored, and oneself, as believer, represents this image in palimpsest, which changes according to the cycle of double death and double life.

Thus, according to a religious saying (followed by theology, theo-philosophy, and mysticism), resurrection could not be conducted by the operation of art. It is needless to insist on the adverse effect, that in its unconscious impulses, intentions and associations, art always remains a dangerous operation, ruinous for all notions of transcendence and invisibility. Art, precisely, reverses, shifts, overturns absence in the materiality of the works; it transforms them into an even more powerful dream, because it relies on the power of nature and the energy of the body. And this dream is to fabricate, to watch oneself work as dream, to produce oneself multiplied in one's simulacra. That is why—and I am merely pointing out this proposition—art requires a double thought, that which accompanies it in its process of elaboration and that which addresses it in its inordinate limits, where, becoming unreason and ruthless disorder, art is the absence of work.

What god between the dream and art? In this case, religion would be an invention of art, a hallucinated universe it would have fashioned, consecrating it to the glory of its wonder, in order to perpetuate the life of humans in a waking dream, a spiritual wonderland. Had that been the case (in the imaginary, it is as true as any play of simulacra), what would then be—with respect to the believer—this fanciful substitution? Monumental substitution, extending far beyond the question of aniconistic monotheism.

Let us return to the mosaic. It revolves around its evanescent center. Hence this vertiginous quality, vertigo of symmetry that I shall discuss below. In every sentence, I would like to turn by turning from this mosaic, like the Orphic gaze, which, moving toward the light and above petrified beauty, has to *sing* forever and ever the prayer of vision. Perhaps we shall have to continue to call "the beautiful" this transfigured conflict of life and death, this instant not of somewhat entropic immortality, but of a deliverance, an energy to live by dint of surviving. Who knows! Perhaps it is this, our eternity—our own.

Artificial vertigo, as I said, that mosaic, that symmetry of the vortex condensed up to the central orthogonal point, that mosaic where the question of "decorative" art should be retained. Decorative art asserts the *doxa* whenever the symbolization of the work is lost, being no longer present in the obviousness, the immediate transparency of a meaning and a clarity of mind. A mosaic, for instance, a carpet, an embroidered scarf, a piece of pottery with geometric designs, think about it! There is nothing, they say, that is worth it, meaning, worth a spiritual exercise that can be applied to masterpieces.

It is something like this that one utters before the rather opaque silence of those simple objects, insignificant adornments. And yet, it is on the basis of this insignificance that one should channel the mind toward an artificial vertigo, where the truth of meaning enters into silence. I will turn slowly at first, in the manner of whirling dervishes. Remember this dance, this haunting obsession, and this gyration that capture the mystical ordeal of the body. Specter of the spiral, and in all its forms. I call upon this metaphor without sharing the ideology of the mystics, but I take it as a lesson, experience of a sensual delight, of a gyrating thought. That is why I call "artificial vertigo" the manifestation of an active thought, which applies itself to the exorcism of its enchantment, its confusions, its breakdowns. Art is its subject, its fiction.

Enlightening fiction, but this experience of the mosaic must mark a certain archeological delineation, despite the fact that every beginning of art is improbable. It has been argued by Islamic art historians[9] that the literary Arabic word *fusayfisa*, mosaics, comes from the Greek language via Aramaic, and that it was designated by the beautiful name of *Constantinopolitan*. Beyond this naming, what comes out of these exegeses is this insistence of the origin and the symbolic. For instance the Islamic mosaics of Byzantine and Greco-Roman inspiration—in them, we perceive an adaptation to the aniconistic mind of Islam, the erasure of animate characters, and the whole thing radicalized into an absolute geometrism, arabesque itself.

At first, green landscape in its most stylized forms will dominate the compositions, before it later opens itself up to an advent of the miniature, Asiatic painting par excellence. What is remarkable, says the art historian, is the diversion of this total geometrism by Christian symbolism. Such diversion of one god by another—the one, though invisible, is embodied in the world of art, while the other, Allah, is forever invisible on earth. The esoteric ingenuity of Christian craftsmen would, from the very beginning, simulacrize Islamic mosaics. A well-known example given by these historians is The Dome of the Rock, its mosaics, reversed or upright hearts symbolizing the heart of Christ and his blood, or those twelve rhombuses in the central lotus, number of apostles—or yet again the Trinity, the motifs of the vase, the ciborium, announcing the mystery of the Holy Grail. And the *rosace*? Renan, the theologian of interfaith interactions (in favor of Christianity), has already answered in his *Philosophie de l'art*, "The rosace, with its diamond petals, depicts the eternal rose, of which all redeemed souls are the leaves."[10] Rose, *rosace*, we shall come back to this flora of arabesques. But for the moment let us consider the following suggestion by Mallarmé: "As to the flowers (. . .) they are, are they not, imitations, artificial, and made to play mosaics."[11]

To construct a perfect and total symmetry? This is what the *rosace* wants, that which becomes ours through rigorously ordered rotation—circles, star polygons, arrows projected toward the center or freeing themselves from its grip, all sorts of forms chiseled and cut with precision, and what an amazing double movement of the circle! What a vortex, what an artifice for a willing thought! And is it not true that thought too, emerging out of the chaos of impressions and emotions besetting it, must submit to the pursuit of symmetry, or rather of a series of symmetries that recall the patterns of nature? How to think symmetrically? What symmetry of art is at stake when the artist impresses upon his body the break with the supposedly raw material of nature? With what notions of symmetry, asymmetry, and dissymmetry must he elevate his works to the principle of a convention? I mean here a nonconvenient convention, the elaboration of an artificial vertigo, the *rosace* in its emergence.

The curious stylist that was Roger Caillois reminds us the following: "Asymmetry, the state that precedes the establishment of an equilibrium, in the instance of a symmetry; and dissymmetry, the state that follows the breaking of an equilibrium or of a symmetry, while letting one speculate on or induce the forsaken order, which is to say, by emerging clearly as a subsequent intervention, subversion that has become necessary or premeditated modification."[12] He distinguishes three types of symmetry—by rotation, by translation, and mirror symmetry. What we have said on the mosaic falls under rotation: "When a given figure turns around a fixed point and successively occupies one or several positions, regularly spaced around the circle, in which it remains identical to itself. Such symmetry may be seen in the arms of a starfish, the figures on modern playing cards (. . .), or the motif repeated around a rose-window, which, if the rose is turned the requisite number of degrees around the center, will coincide precisely with the preceding or following one. On a plane, rotation around a fixed center thus divides the space into equal sections, in which the same pattern reappears at regular intervals. Once again, each image is superposable on the next one, simply by slipping."[13]

Without directly worrying about what Caillois means by "the total syntax of the universe," I shall stress—with respect to the artificial vertigo—two points in his account: on the one hand, considering that art is exorcism of madness, and on the other, it carries out, that said, a celebration of symmetry, according to Caillois's suggestions: "In any case, he (man) has shifted so strongly to the side of dissymmetry that symmetry appears to him as a kind of ultimate safeguard when, compromised, his ability to perceive or reason is stricken by vertigo. The recourse to symmetry then becomes a lifeline to which the patient clings: threatened to slide into chaos, he sees it as the last perceptible manifestation of the regularity of the universe. He takes refuge, away from the turmoil of life, in an active geometrization and mechanization. Symmetry releases him from the absurdity that consumes him."[14]

Let us go back to the question. The mosaic forms an artificial rose (*warda*), a *rosace*. Look at a diagram of this flower—an exercise known to the mosaicist as well as the botanist—you will see the hint of an *in-between*, between the rose and the *rosace*, between nature and the technique of art. Surely the diagram of a rose is already a *rosace*, which contemplates itself by rotating on its axis. Rhythm, mobility— symmetry rests on the necessity of the invariant, but it rests just as much on the *variation of the invariant*, vibration of those patterns that could be designated by *a polygraphic rhetoric*: geometrism, ribs, mirrors, reversals, connections, and embedments. Add the play of colors, and you will get a spiritual garland offered to the eye.

What artifice gives form to this double of the rose that no longer produces the natural shape of a flower, but *stylizes* it? Take this word in its connotations and effects, the whole procession of its referents and signs, which we can weave according to its specters. Why, for what reason and unreason, am I led to return to the artificial vertigo brought about by the gaze of a *rosace*? Based on which *understanding* of evanescence—between me and me? What would be the act of this haunting obsession? One would have to keep writing with every trace of this vertigo, this silent cry, in the face of any abysmal question.

Clearly, the *rosace* eliminates the boundary between the inside and the outside of a flower, between its maturation and blossoming. An operation that Hegel mentions in the beginning of his *Phenomenology of Spirit* about the floral dialectic through the transformed order of its successive repressions, and which, moreover, has made Derrida write differently in that singular masterpiece that *Glas* will always be, namely, for instance, that "the flower opens out, achieves, consecrates the phenomenon of death in an instant of *trance*."[15] Strange *jouissance* through which what gives itself to be seen in its appearance is this loss of consciousness it undergoes by simulating it. Simulacrum of an explosion, a blossoming, the *rosace* itself. When it brings about the vertigo, this mosaic holds in itself a language of unconsciousness, transportation, and deadly trance. The mosaic looks at me as irradiated stone—statufying me. Before the abyss.

For instance, the offering of a strange bouquet whose petals are completely open, disclosed, deflowering themselves by means of hermaphroditic insemination. Besides, imagine the work of the craftsman who, hammer in hand, cuts with great precision. Mosaic—symmetry that turns by turning away from its axis, from the invariant of its chiseled order.

It is also true that this whole story of cutting and even beheading can be told according to a *hadith* reported by the theologian Ibn Abbas, to whom a Persian artist had asked, "But will I not be able to draw animals anymore? Will I not be able to practice my craft?—You can, but only if you can cut off the heads of the animals so that they do not look alive, and try to make it so that they resemble flowers."[16] Yes, what an agony of resemblance and *mimesis* for the artist to fulfill the theological duty.

But if the flower *is not of life*, what is it then in representations? Inanimate thing, thinks the theologian. However, due to his ignorance, these words provide a certain clarification—the *rosace* in Islamic art could only be represented in its decorative futility, more or less than a rose doomed to inertia, to the dissolution of all symmetry, matter itself according to modern science. Let us then arrest this gesture of the theologian, this fascination of decapitation, already so well written between the rose and Genet in Derrida's *Glas*. Let us arrest it, cut it otherwise? Rose, *rosace*—an analogy? Rather an agglutination of two names, two orders, that of nature and that of art. And we are no further forward here if we consider the one (the *rosace*) as the metaphor of the other (rose, *warda*) by continuously reversing the terms of the analogy, their mirroring games. A systematically geometrical, arithmetic, and symbolic analysis is not more pertinent either. We would rather say that it is a question of a dissymmetry occurring in a combinatorial symmetry such that the artificial vertigo is the simulacrum of a haunting obsession that strives to exorcise itself, to come back constantly to its enchantments. Enchantment, a magical question of art, its tie to the impossible.

We symbolize differently. *Rosace*—Mystical Rose, as we have repeatedly said, where Islam, precisely, does not symbolize in the same way the sign of the flower by giving it only the grace—it is already so admirable—of an insignificant, inert ornament, stylized pattern of a barely recognizable nature, subtle fervor of an appearance with no life represented, labor of an artisanal production. But when it becomes pure geometrism, decorative plant and interlacing of calligraphy, we say it is an *arabesque*. Arabesque? Word of European origin, *zakhrafa* in Arabic (idea of ornament), but what is remarkable in this gyration, these repetitions, palmettes and calyxes in pairs of forked leaves, these cartouches and medallions, these embedded calligrams, it is this ability of the leaf and the stem, in a way pushing one into the other with a relentless regularity, as if the regularly repeated vine and its stylization called for our spiritual intoxication, our willingness of thought.

This movement has made the heads of Islamic art historians spin, those who are in love with the esoteric and mysticism. Yet we no longer symbolize with the same mind-sets. Our spiral—writing word—follows a different trajectory, an other-thought. But I so much wish to give this bouquet of symbols a eulogy that is the glorification we owe to the dead covered with wild plants.

> I therefore leave open the question of arabesque and its relationship to the Islamic arts, while I mention in this parenthesis the anecdote that involves this questioning about the *rosace*. I had asked a mosaicist— through a friend, his son—to make this mosaic for me, on the sole condition that he reverse the colors he used for his cartoons. He accepted, but composed two series of enameled tiles: one (his) with the usual colors, and the other (the one I requested) with the desired reversal, it being understood that the form was to remain the same in both cases. After a long hesitation, he made the *rosace* as I wanted. I think he made another one with the other tiles, for himself or somebody else. I gave him a copy of the Quran. Had I tricked God a little bit? What incalculable gift, what (false) gift have we given ourselves, especially when I think of my paternal grandfather, a dead person I had never seen, and who was also a mosaicist?

I speak, traveling through Islamic art. And although writing works against speech by realizing it otherwise and turning it away from its immediacy, at a conference open to the risks of art, it is better to *speak by writing*. Another name of this itinerary, while all I do, by going back and forth past the edifices, mosaics, and miniatures, is choose artworks— such minor ones at first glance. Let us then let our propositions weave together as we go along.

Wandering question. I remember, during a stay in Damascus, the powerful attraction imposed on me by the great Umayyad Mosque (Figure 6.2). Every time I walked through the ancient town, I would find myself brought back to its glowing trails. I entered, seized by an emotion that had moved me from a distance. Emotion that sprung forth, no doubt, from the splendor of this complex and eccentric architecture, eccentric on account of being transformed with the historical and

Figure 6.2 Umayyad Mosque, Damascus (prayer hall)

religious changes, as if paganism and monotheism were enriched by
an excess of ever more additional artistic motifs. I turned. The *minbar*
(pulpit) and *mihrab* (which indicates the direction of Mecca) were, are,
in their proper direction, while the axis of my vortex (of fascination)
made me deviate toward a kind of silent, unpronounceable prayer. The
entire architecture of this mosque, at first a church after having been
the site of a pagan cult, this whole ceremony, this procession of gods led
me irresistibly toward two more discreet places—the place reserved for
women for prayer, which is lightly protected by a parapet (a carved veil
between the gaze of the two sexes), and then, in front of a saint's tomb
(February 1980) where I saw an old man getting into trance, magnetized
by an increasingly jerky movement against the marble. Which god was
calling me? What presence of the invisible for the one who, like me,
only wants to see what manifests itself in the vision of stone, searching
myself, dreaming myself as I walked, as this edifice—ostentatious in
all respects—raised in my imaginary the form of a fiction. Everything
became so captivating when I was shown, outside the great prayer hall
I just mentioned, another, tiny room. In there I was shown a black
hole, surrounded by cloth (I think) and where the women, especially,
murmured some Quranic verses, laying their hands in front of the
black hole. Hole that contains, they say, the severed head of Husayn
the martyr. But we also know that such holes exist in Iraq and Iran as
well. Severed head, wandering from century to century, according to
the repeated sacrifice of the Shias.

I shall for a moment remain in this symbolic gape where religion is
overtaken by the art of the mosque, art that works for its own account in
the movement of its fantasy and its constructs. Since time immemorial,
paganism and its cults have been celebrations of the image, of idols.
Celebrations that Abrahamic theology has transgressed by the law of the
One, the Name, and the Text. I shall maintain between art and religion
this irreducible movement of two fictions erasing one another in favor
of what remains there in front of the gaze. And it is these remainders—
these remnants—these trails to be deciphered in mosques, palaces, and
all objects produced under the impetus of Islam, it is therefore these

remains that undermine, in their own way, the notions of invisibility and absolute absence by giving them back to the reality of all presence. About these remainders—Hegel declared that art is a thing of the past, belongs to the past. It should be kept in mind that theology, at times enemy of art, at others its guardian, is itself of the past, ideology and architectonics of a world giving the visible to the invisible, the body of the believer to its hallucinations, of which we shall see a miniature later on, that of *Al-Burāq*, the fabulous animal that carries the prophet Muhammad to the sky, up to heaven.

And without waiting too long—scansion of a nomad questioning— we can ask ourselves without any piece of mind, any torment either, of the infinite waiting, we can ask this: What is a product of heavenly art? And heaven itself, metaphor of eternal bliss, death itself, the work of mourning in the decaying corpse, not becoming invisible but being eaten and torn by piercing decomposing matter, spiritual inertia of believers and theologians, whereas, dead, they dream of heaven. Without really riding with this fabulous being *Al-Burāq*, neither woman nor mule (what a phantasm, what a fantastic blend of religious alchemy!), without yet rising with the metaphor of heaven or bringing it down into the simplicity of a vision, we risk falling outside certain frameworks in which art had been kept, like an either glorious or pointless, mundane illustration, a way of dressing the profane world in fineries, disguises doomed to be destroyed before the invisibility of God. On the basis of this double procession—from art to theology—let us decide.

First, on a nontheological level. You recall this major argument: only Allah creates, whereas the artist cannot imitate Him in the construction of any simulacrum by producing a reproduction, an imitation of the miraculous act, since God configured, says the theologian, the Whole in its absolute diversity and its infinite forms. How would the artist be capable of expressing its ultimate perfection? Every beginning, every decision of an act of creation belongs, comes back to this law and the law of all beginnings that engender everything in its nature and its supernature. Every principle of beginning is a principle of creation, attributed only to its creator, the One, the non-begotten. Creator, which has neither beginning nor end, being defined by no resemblance, no human quality.

That is why theological discourse cannot imagine two heavens—that of religion and that of art. And when he imagines the unfulfilled *jouissances* in him, the theologian cannot but *downgrade* art by separating it from its power of simulation—heaven, hell, theories of angles and *houris*, landscapes that parade in this forceful repression would be invisible on this earth. This is how the Law is its own heaven in image, when, in a mosque, in a sanctuary, in the solitude of the soul, the believer *has to pray* for his exorcism, he prays to God to release him from himself, from his body, his terrible urges, he begs him to give him the pure image of a disembodiment. We cannot really understand the position of theology—with respect to the image—if we do not lay bare this divine torture, this submission to the Law turned toward heaven, a law announcing an invisible reward for him (his death), this "wager on immortality," which is to say for art the form of a name and a corpse striving to become invisible, to decompose in the redemption of the never-seen, never-enjoyed.

Yes, curious adventure of aniconism, and I do not forget, this said, my walking in Damascus, this mosque that carves in prayer to die from it, to become its spiritual stone in a lacework of metaphors now—for us—obsolete. What is the difference between a mosque and the heavenly call as I turned in the intoxication of *my* unbelievable? I shall barely describe this mosque, because, precisely, heaven belongs to the order of the indescribable, the improbable. Hidden, veiled, sewn to the body, to the phallus turned toward heaven, Islamic *jouissance* hoodwinks itself, with the perpetual iteration of the One, the Name, and the Text.

Let us put it straightforwardly—this stone that is erected in the imaginary, in its heavenly production according to the torment of the living body, is an extreme paradigm of theological power, its destruction, as well as its self-destruction. A *mihrab*, they say, shows the direction of the Kaaba, then follows the phantasmagoria of *Rabi'a al-'Adawiyya*, old flute player and convert to mysticism, follows her as she declares, "Now the Kaaba comes to meet me."

Being only one example among others, this ambivalence ties mysticism to theology, without raising here the question of Islamic theo-philosophy. Let us go on, keeping in mind the image of heaven that passes through, goes into trances, by way of an edifice, a stone, a mosque, a marabout sanctuary with or without a dome, as well as the severed head of Husayn or the animal that Ibn Abbas talks about, animal transfigurable into a flower. I am, always, on the side of the flower, the stone, the impregnable thing, and of every behind-the-scenes where the metaphysics of art founders. Let us go back to the story of the great mosque of Damascus. A mosque, says history, built in place of an ancient temple dedicated to Jupiter. After the triumph of Christianity, the statue of this god fell, and a place of offering to John the Baptist was erected in the perimeter of the church, also dedicated to Herodias's murder. Yet another story of a tête-à-tête. I must have remembered this story as I stepped into the mosque; otherwise how do I juxtapose the martyrdom of Husayn and that of John the Baptist, this procession of holes, mystical gapings, and severed heads?

And yet, acknowledges the historian, there was a problem of sharing the temple between Islam and Christianity. It was therefore divided into two parts separated by a wall. Afterward, it was completely occupied by the Muslims—hence the evolution of the mosque. Let us go back to the prayer hall from where I turned, in a way, with my head, following those mosaics, those gilded and polychrome-pierced walls, those stain glass windows as well, and those immense columns—Greco-Roman and Byzantine style on the whole, with some modifications due to Islam. Also remarkable are the four *mihrabs* (doctrinal number), the naves parallel to the *Qibla*, whose axial vessel led the great Orientalist of art A. Papadopoulo to write, "The axial vessel, through its opposition to the three naves parallel to the *Qibla*, realizes perfectly the required contrast of its role of mystical compass needle that a mosque is."[17] Very well! Let us walk yet a little longer in this hall of slightly rectangular structure, and take flight—in the Greek sense of *metaphora*, transportation.

And this flight will be illustrated by a third image, a magnificent Persian miniature representing the prophet Muhammad mounted on

Al-Burāq. The sixteenth-century miniature from the Safavid period (according to the poems of Nizami Ganjavi) one can admire either in the standard reproductions or at the British Museum (Figure 6.3).

This choice, in memory of a paradise, of an unforgettable image, if we accept that heaven recalls here a wandering metaphor. But we should also instantly recall the narrative. It is said in the first verse of the seventeenth surah of the Quran entitled *Isra* (*The Night Journey*), "Glory to the One who carried his Servant by night from the Sacred Mosque to the farthest Mosque, whose surroundings We have blessed, to make him see some of Our signs. He is the All-hearer, the All-seer."[18] Here a few remarks should be made. The verb *asra'a* means to take someone on a journey, to carry someone by night. The Sacred Mosque designates, according to the exegesis, the temple of Mecca. But where is the Farthest Mosque? In Jerusalem, it is generally asserted. However, it seems that this explanation was preceded by another, that of the making of the Prophet—an explanation that includes this journey, not as a miracle, but as a simple vision, a hallucination when, asleep at home or near the Kaaba, Muhammad sees himself taken in his mind. But popular imagination, including that of the artists, was fascinated rather by the phantasmagoria of a real ascent to the sky. Hence the figure of this fabulous animal, whose strange and perhaps foreign name would come from the Persian *būraq* (steed), and recalls at the same time, through phonetic agglutination, the Arabic word *barq* (lightning). Either way, the name is used both in the feminine and the masculine, always with the definite article.

I cannot possibly recount before you all the descriptions imagined by the most orthodox theologians, without mentioning a popular and so rich a fable. This beast, both horse and mule, or half-woman (only the head) and the other part a kind of flying mule. "Impossible," writes S. C. Welch, "to imagine a more beautiful Islamic religious image,"[19] about this miniature whose reproduction I have here before me. And by talking, letting my fantasy come and go according to a heavenly nostalgia, I feel as if I were going back in time, idly, in an order that—though enchanted—presents itself in the guise of a willing thought.

Figure 6.3 Buraq (sixteenth-century miniature)

For, looking at the whole miniature where the Prophet rises toward the sky, I do not know where to begin, or where to begin again—so much splendor, so much fantasy that rivals so wonderfully the greatest finds of Arabic and Islamic painting. The spiraling movement is noticed at the first glance. All the characters, in their different stases, do not seem to turn their body around the Prophet, but they themselves are the emanation, the radiation of so many rays of a light that takes its flight, a light that is at once moving and still, a lightning, golden flame of those over-rich—improbable—colors.

Let us focus on Muhammad and Buraq for a moment. Muhammad is looking toward the left of the miniature, where the archangel Gabriel, in the return of the gaze, indicates to him the celestial path, and it is with the gesture of the slightly raised left hand that Muhammad responds. Embellished by all sorts of waistbands and garments in the form of light, Gabriel shows no trace of his legs and feet: rich lacework of contrasted colors, a matching gesture of the hand, blue and red wings, which, driven by arabesque, "touch" straight to the "foot," the "hoof"—so to speak—of Buraq.

Undeniably, this fabulous being has the head of a woman, a Mongolian woman, like all the characters, except for the very Semitic face of the Prophet. Buraq does not have wings, but owing to its improbable form, "she" in a way bears the weight of the gyratory movement. So here it is, the head with a crown of gold, the oblique gaze, the strand of hair around the left ear ending with a bright red dot (a precious stone, I gather); below the neckline, an indeterminable ornament, whose strongly curved fringes reveal an asexual chest, an impersonal flesh. A woman's head, certainly, but that is all; as to the rest, delicate hooves, so delicate (a dancing move in the middle of the sky) and bent in a play of lace; the entire armature of the body, plain and uniform, is covered with embroideries and a little saddle cloth; finally, the tail pulling it toward the wing of an angel. Everywhere angels fly. I see them, at the bottom of the miniature, two by two—scenes of love in the sky.

One would have to follow this reverie to honor this art, this divine love of stasis in ecstasy. These angels turned toward one another are remarkable in that (I am still talking about the scene at the bottom) no smile, mouth closed, but visible offering, and even desiring gestures of the hands, disrupted gestures, all this is necessary so that physical contact does not become, through calligraphy, calligraphic medallions transcribing Nizami's *Khamsa*, his mystical collection of poems. The angel's love at a distance, the painting itself of this miniature— as if, disguising his desires, the artist awakened in us the *paradise of our body*.

Paradise and its hell—in the miniature, this praying martyr, and we do not know whether he is praying before the veiled sun right in front of him or whether, cut off from his wings, he remains tied to his suffering, pinned to the sky. Perhaps this impression is freely suggested to me by this picture in clouds—clouds or fragmentary dragons, it does not matter which. This other martyr—his garland waistbands turn around in the form of snakes to face the veiled sun. To bite what? What fantastic and incredible evil? And what of this female angel, bare-breasted (the only one) and who, placed below, between Gabriel and Buraq, holds in her hands a straight red line, passing over the archangel's thigh, then falling back in the form of a candelabrum (?). Everything turns. One can look at this miniature starting from any point in space. Tremendous skill of the artist and of his imaginary topography—the sky would be this night journey, this ascension of Islamic art to heaven, in which it grounds itself in spirit. I do not know what name to give to this remarkable nakedness of the chest and of a foot, just one, sexualizing—for me—the body of an entirely earthly *houri*. This body is dressed with its wings, its red dress, yet again garland waistbands and two bracelets (one at each wrist), and what an erect red line!

Let us end with that procession of angels and messengers around the Prophet. Are they carrying heavenly food? Fruits? And even a book? Procession of metaphors, which I would not want to reduce to their use for the realization of this night journey, but this miniature, whose analysis seems to me never-ending (my heavenly desire has its weaknesses, its limits), is exceptional in Islamic art.

Three images taken as example—among others—to present Islamic art, and with some liberty, insofar as the latter matches the gravity of the question, "what about art?"

I shall confine myself to making a few remarks. I indicate two paths for research—one is archeological, and the other, directed toward actuality. Complementary paths. Their relationship depends on the manner in which the researcher comes into play. The archeological path aims to analyze Islamic art with respect to its classical (theological, theo-philosophical, mystical, scientific) *episteme*. And we know that there is no global aesthetics in this episteme, that the notion of "art" itself was conveyed by *sinā'a*, manufacture—*sinā'a ach-chi'r* for instance, which means poetic fabrication, and that the different disciplines that had dealt with art have done so on a regional basis, without developing a global, total, and universal domain, corresponding to what is called, in the West, aesthetics.

This archaeological site is of great significance, provided that it is cleared on the basis of a dual approach—that of the deciphering of already established discourses about this or that art, such as music in the thought of Al-Farabi, poetics according to the grammarians. Deciphering that is also to be carried out according to the accomplished works of artists, work that always precedes its maker, its producer. Arab criticism, as well as Orientalism, has neglected this relationship between the discourse and the work, the fabrication and the object fabricated. Negligence, which is not a negligence in a way, because this distinction is a foundation of Islamic metaphysics.

The archaeological stage, which is always beginning again, is decisive in an other-thought. But now that the notions of art, aesthetics, and work are subjected to a radical critique, on the one hand, and that, on the other, they are faced with the expansion of the techniques of reproduction (audiovisual notably), our questions should be formulated adequately to the situation. The reproduction of the image wipes out the idea of the original and the copy, and thus introduces a new serial order, a mass fabrication of copies without original, fabrication that is carried out according to the immediate needs and their rapidity. Such a reproduction shakes our traditional and too "literary" perception of art, its metaphysics, and its theology.

All across the Arab world, the image reproduced for any purpose (domestic, sociopolitical, cultural) makes the debate surrounding aniconism in Islam obsolete. And thus begins another interrogation between the reproduction of the image and its traditional representation, between this new visible and the invisibility of a now veiled God. To give just one very striking example in Arab films, the extreme inertness of the objects that make up the décor. A particular chair is far from being a dramatic element, a rhythmic point in the film—that chair *does not act*; it does not play its role; it just sits there in the conventional, excessive way, without any solid connection to the logic of the narrative. That chair in image does not allow the characters to be drawn to it on account of its different ritual postures, all of which are movements through which it lets itself be sit upon, taken, or thrown out of the window. What do we see? A *moved* object, in other words, an object that does not have its site in the dramatic topography. Nonexistent presence of objects and things, which is symptomatic in Arab cinema. It requires, in order to be brought to light, the elucidation of tremendous questions on the simulacra of vision in an age of perpetual reproduction. To my knowledge, this kind of analysis does not seem to be a concern for film criticism in the Arab countries.

That is why we ask the same question: What about contemporary art? What about Arab and Islamic art between its actuality and inactuality?

(1982)

Notes

1 Other-Thought

This article put forward here is a new version of the one I published as part of a collaborative work entitled *Du Maghreb* (in *Les Temps modernes* [Paris, October 1977]).

This collaborative work came out at a time when the Maghreb was already involved in the Saharan conflict, on which I had taken a personal position that did not conform to those of the Maghreb States (cf. *Le Monde*, September 2–3, 1979).

This political engagement spoke for itself, relaying the theoretical propositions that I had presented in various studies.

This book consists of a series of papers. Some are hitherto unpublished, while others have already been published on various occasions. I dated every article in order to maintain the continuity *and* the discontinuity of the book. I take fully and unreservedly upon myself the points of failure and incompletion. Since these papers have been written at different times and in varied circumstances, I have respected the writing style of each. I think the important thing is to identify the questions and their (critical and polemical) formulation on this name that the Maghreb gives itself.

I have limited these questions to five themes, in relation to the text that opens the book. The first theme concerns the sociological discourse (and the discourse of social sciences) on the Maghreb, as I apply my analysis to the sole example of precolonial hierarchy.

This first theme justifies the passage to the second, which is a polemical critique of Orientalism, or rather of a certain Orientalism flourishing in the Maghreb.

And if I have also concentrated on the other themes (bilingualism, sexuality, art), it is with the same aim of trying to open up research in the Maghreb to those silent questions, repressed by the theological order and by the order of scientism.

I tried to take my examples especially from Morocco. Exclusion? Lack of information: No, rather the specification of a place inscribed in a plural Maghreb, whence the words to come would take this text over by giving it up to its erasure.

1 Translator's Note (T.N. hereafter). Frantz Fanon, *The Wretched of the Earth*, trans. Constance Farrington (New York: Grove Weidenfeld, 1963), 311.

2 T.N. Throughout the book, I have chosen to render *actualité* and *inactualité* by "actuality" and "inactuality" for convenience, but "actuality" should be read as the state of that which is present, the present situation as a whole and current events, and "inactuality" as the state of bearing no relation to actuality.

3 T.N. "Between Hellenism and Renaissance: Islam, the Intermediate Civilization," in *Islamic Studies 2*, 1963. Citation taken from Mohammed Arkoun, *Essais sur la pensée Islamique* (Paris: Maison-neuve et Larose, 1973).

4 T.N. Friedrich Nietzsche, *The Portable Nietzsche*, ed. and trans. Walter Kaufmann (New York: Penguin, 1977), 652.

5 Cf. Abdallah Laroui, *Idéologie arabe contemporaine* (Paris: Maspero, 1967), 19. T.N. All translations from this book are mine.

6 Cf. his book *Livre des pénétrations métaphysiques*, translated by Henri Corbin (Paris, 1954). T.N. For an English translation, see Mulla Sadra, *Book of Metaphysical Penetrations*, trans. Seyyed Hussein Nasr, ed. Ibrahim Kalin (Provo, UT: Brigham Young University Press, 2014).

7 Laroui, *Idéologie arabe contemporaine*, 15.

8 T.N. A term commonly translated as "authenticity" or "originality," and which I have rendered here as "originarity," following the author's remark in the third chapter concerning the rendering of this term by "authenticity." He deems this translation incorrect and suggests *originarité* as a more adequate translation. For a further discussion on the meaning of this term that takes account of this difference, I refer the reader to *Among the Jasmine Trees: Music and Modernity in Contemporary Syria* (Jonathan Holt Shannon, Middletown, CT: Wesleyan University Press, 2006), 57–58.

9 Heraclitus, Fragment in *A Presocratic Reader*, 2nd ed., ed. Patricia Curd, trans. Richard D. McKirahan and Patricia Curd (Indianapolis, IN: Hackett, 2011), 50.

2 Double Critique

1   T.N. Arthur Rimbaud, *A Season in Hell and The Drunken Boat*, trans. Louise Varèse (New York: New Directions, 2011), 73.

2   We borrow this notion from Jacques Derrida, insofar as (1) his thought is also a dialogue with the "surpassing of metaphysics"—a critical and affirmative thought that elaborates, step by step, a thought of difference, between philosophy, science, and writing; and (2) *deconstruction*, as the unhinging of Western metaphysics and as driven by Derrida, in his rather singular way, accompanied *decolonization* in its historical occurrence. We note here some nonfortuitous outcomes of this encounter—the encounter between decolonization and deconstruction.

3   Karl Marx and Friedrich Engels, *The Marx-Engels Reader*, ed. Robert C. Tucker (New York: W.W. Norton & Company, 1978), 659.

4   Cf. our pamphlet *Bilan de la sociologie au Maroc* (Rabat: Publications de l'Association pour la recherche en sciences humaines, 1967).

5   Georges Hardy, *Les elements de l'Histoire Coloniale* (Paris: La Renaissance du Livre, 1920). T.N. Translation is mine.

6   Jacques Derrida, "Structure, Sign and Play in the Discourse of the Human Sciences," in *Writing and Difference*, trans. Alan Bass (Chicago, IL: University of Chicago Press, 1978), 282.

7   Cf. my study on "bilingualism and literature" in the present book.

8   Cf. translation of *Prolegomena* into French by Vincent Monteil; Ibn Khaldun, *Al-Muqaddima: Discours sur l'histoire universelle*, trans. V. Monteil (Sindbad: Beirut, 1968), 75 [*The Muqaddimah: An Introduction to History* (Abridged Edition), ed. N. J. Dawood, trans. Franz Rosenthal (Princeton, NJ: Princeton University Press, 2015)]. T.N. All translations from this book are mine.

9   Ibid., 77.

10 Ibid., 62.

11 On the problem of a homology between historical mutations and mutations of the discourses, cf. Julia Kristeva, *Desire in Language: A Semiotic Approach to Literature and Art* (Oxford: Blackwell, 1980).

12 Needless to say, this "universal history" is but the universe he knew of. One cannot blame Ibn Khaldun for having ignored countless

civilizations. His is not an encyclopedic project, but well and truly a discourse on history.

13 This proposition is ambiguous, because theology is not a science—a science that would have God as its object is impossible to found. Cf. H. Hanafi, "Théologie ou anthropologie," paper delivered at the conference "la Renaissance du Monde Arabe," November 1970, Louvain, Belgium.

14 Nassif Nassar, *La pensée réaliste d'Ibn Khaldûn* (Paris: PUF, 1967). T.N. Translation is mine.

15 Ibn Khaldun, *Al-Muqaddima*, 85. An old idea, so dear to Aristotle and to Hellenist Arab philosophers. Cf. J. Berque, "Problèmes de la connaissance au temps d'Ibn Khaldûn," in *Contributions à la sociologie de la connaissance*, prefaced by Roger Bastide (Paris: Anthropos, 1967).

16 We are obviously thinking here of Claude Lévi-Strauss. Although Khaldunian thought lends itself to a certain structural analysis, Ibn Khaldun remains a theorist of macro-history after all.

17 Ibn Khaldun, *Al-Muqaddima*, 87.

18 Ibid., 88.

19 Ibid., 89.

20 Otherwise, the extremely complicated structure of *Prolegomena* would be illegible. In the first chapter, for instance, Ibn Khaldun looks at cosmogonic geography, divinatory tables, prophecy, astrology, dreams, and more. An essentially thematic analysis would miss the originality of this thought, which requires a plural reading.

21 In addition to the classic studies of Mircea Eliade, see the exceptional analysis of such an underestimated thinker, Pierre Klossowski, *Nietzsche and the Vicious Circle*, trans. Daniel W. Smith (Chicago, IL: University of Chicago Press, 1998) [*Nietzsche et le cercle vicieux* (Paris: Mercure de France, 1969)].

22 Unfortunately, the typology elaborated by Georges Gurvitch does not help us very much: *La multiplicité des temps sociaux* (Paris: CDU, 1958).

23 We readily adopt N. Nassar's translation, which seems more appropriate to us, in Nassar, *La pensée ré aliste d'Ibn Khaldûn* (Paris: PUF, 1967).

24 Ibn Khaldun, *Al-Muqaddima*, 273.

25 Nassar, *La pensée réaliste d'Ibn Khaldûn*, 181–191.

26 Ibn Khaldun, *Al-Muqaddima*, 302.

27 Ibid., 253.

28 Ibid., 266.

29 "Every client belongs to the group (of his patrons), whether he be client through slavery (*riqq*), through artifice (*içtina*), or through alliance." T.N. Translation is mine.

30 Ibid., 277.

31 Ibid., 365.

32 Ibid., 599.

33 Ibid., 482.

34 Ibid., 800.

35 Ibid., 801.

36 The following paragraphs are partly inspired by Abdel Aziz Belal, "Sur la pensée économique d'Ibn Khaldûn," *Bulletin économique et social du Maroc*, vol. 30, no. 108 (1968), 3–11.

37 Ibid., 6. T.N. Translation is mine.

38 Ibn Khaldun, *Al-Muqaddima*, 801–802.

39 Abdallah Laroui, *The History of the Maghrib: An Interpretive Essay*, trans. Ralph Manheim (Princeton, NJ: Princeton University Press, 2015), 156. [*Histoire du Maghreb* (Paris: Maspero, 1970), 212.]

40 Whose most popular representative is E. F. Gautier. Cf. *Les Siècles obscurs du Maghreb* (Paris: Payot, 1927).

41 It is remarkable to observe that it is an Arab thinker who takes on board the notion of "colonizability" (cf. Malek Bennabi, *Vocation de l'islam* [Paris: Le Seuil, 1954] [*Islam in History and Society*, trans. Asma Rashid (New Delhi: Kitab Bhavan, 1999)]). Either "colonizability" refers to the endogenous crisis of a society, crisis that does not allow it to resist imperial penetration, in which case the analysis has shifted: it is necessary to dismantle the mechanisms of this conjunction between the two facts (endogenous crisis and imperialism). Or the notion of "colonizability" connotes a certain psychology of peoples, which makes a distinction between colonizable and noncolonizable societies, in which case we leave the scientific domain and promote a racist ideology.

42 *Oriental Despotism: A Comparative Study of Total Power* (New Haven, CT: Yale University Press, 1957). [*Le Despotisme oriental: étude comparative du pouvoir total*, trans. Anne Marchand (Paris: Éd. de Minuit, 1964)].

43 Laroui, *The History of the Maghrib*, 146. But already in 1955, J. Berque wrote, "The system of *taqbilt* (tribe) is only intelligible as a consequence. Not only is it influenced by many factors, but it only arises or is conceived in relation to outside or higher entities" (*Structures sociales du Haut Atlas* [Paris: P.U.F., 1955], 442; *Social Structures of the High Atlas*, trans. Jane Bigwood, http://www.worldcat.org/title/social-structures-of-the-high-atlas/oclc/12188187). T.N. All translations from this book are mine.

44 Laroui, *The History of the Maghrib*, 66.

45 Roland Barthes, "Le Discours de l'histoire," *Informations sur les sciences sociales*, vol. 6, no. 4 (August 1967). T.N. Translation is mine.

46 Cf. the works of Paul Pascon.

47 This is a strange paradox for a nationalist who, taking on board certain achievements of Marxism, rejoins the problematic of the liberal "technophile," which he has described in his *Idéologie arabe contemporaine* (Paris: Maspero, 1967).

48 This is an excerpt from a notebook entitled, "Le Système foncier en Algérie au moment de la conquête française," in *Sur les sociétés précapitalistes* (selected texts of Marx-Engels-Lenin), prefaced by M. Godelier (Paris: Éditions sociales, 1970). T.N. All translations from this text are mine.

49 Ibid., 394.

50 Ibid., 390.

51 Ibid., 398–399.

52 Kovalevsky as quoted by Marx, Debates of the National Assembly, 1873. T.N. Translation is mine.

53 Cf. *Sur le mode de production asiatique* (Paris: Éditions sociales, 1969). See also K. Wittfogel, *Oriental Despotism: A Comparative Study of Total Power* (New Haven, CT: Yale University Press, 1957), Chapter IX. Wittfogel, by developing a sociology "deriving" from the cold war, ends up including all state centralization, regardless of the social system that presupposes it, within the general form of what he calls "oriental despotism."

54 "Formen, die der kapitalischen Produktion vorhergehen."

55 *Sur les sociétés précapitalistes* (Paris: Éditions sociales, 1970), 17.

56 Yves Lacoste, *Ibn Khaldoun: Naissance de l'Histoire, passé du tiers monde* (Paris: La Découverte, 1966) [*Ibn Khaldun: The Birth of History and the*

Past of the Third World, trans. David Macey (London: Verso, 1984)], cf. especially the first chapter. T.N. All translations from this book are mine.

57 Ibid., 37.

58 Ibid.

59 The systems of *iqta'* and *hināya* give a right to use, and not to appropriate.

60 Ibid., 36.

61 Ibid., 32.

62 Ibid., 34.

63 René Gallissot, *Sur le féodalisme* (Paris: Éditions sociales, 1971), 158. T.N. All translations from this book are mine.

64 He thus separates himself from the thesis put forward by Robert Montagne, *Les Berbères et le Makhzen* (Paris: Éd. Félix Alcan, 1930) [*The Berbers and the Makhzen in the South of Morocco: Essay on the Political Transformation of the Sedentary Berbers (the Chleuh Group)*, trans. Jean Winchell (New Haven, CT: HRAF, 1995)].

65 Gallissot, *Sur le féodalisme*, 158.

66 Ibid., 176.

67 Ibid., 164.

68 Cf. M. Godelier, "La Pensée de Marx et d'Engels aujourd'hui et les recherches de demain," *La Pensée*, no. 143, Paris, February 1969 ("The Thought of Marx and Engels Today and Tomorrow's Research," *International Journal of Sociology*, vol. 2, nos. 2/3, Structuralism and Marxism: A Debate, Summer-Fall 1972, 133–177). T.N. Translations from this article are mine.

69 M. Mauss, *Essai sur le don* (Paris: Presses Universitaires de France, 2012) [*The Gift: Forms and Functions of Exchange in Archaic Societies*, trans. Ian Cunnison (Eastford: Martino Fine Books, 2011)]. An essay extended by Georges Bataille's brilliant intuitions, which in turn are confirmed by François Perroux. Cf. G. Bataille, *La Part maudite* (Paris: Le Seuil, 1970) [*The Accursed Share: An Essay on General Economy*, trans. Robert Hurley (New York: Zone Books, 1988)].

70 Cf. the collective book *L'Algérie: passé et présent* (Paris: Éditions sociales, 1960). Cf. also Lucette Valensi, *Le Maghreb avant la prise d'Alger* (Paris: Flammarion, 1969). This work of Marxist inspiration, which is rather heterogeneous, ideologically joins colonial sociology in its most questionable analyses.

71 Obviously, Gallissot's study concerns mainly twentieth-century Algeria: there are many documents on this period, whereas Gallissot's analysis needs to be verified on a much more extensive period. Hence the relative scope of this whole discussion.

72 Roger Bastide, *Formes élémentaires de la stratification* (Paris: CDU, 1965).

73 Cf. Georges Balandier, *Anthropologie politique* (Paris: PUF, 1967) [*Political Anthropology*, trans. A. M. Sheridan Smith (Harmondsworth: Penguin Press, 1970)].

74 Cf. *De la division du travail social*, 8e édition (Paris: PUF, 1967), 150 [*The Division of Labor in Society*, trans. W. D. Halls (New York: Simon & Schuster, 1997)]; cf. also R. Maunier, *Sociologie coloniale* (Paris: Domat-Montchrestien, 1936) [*The Sociology of Colonies*, trans. E. O. Lorimer (Oxon: Routledge, 2002)]. T.N. Translation is taken from *Emile Durkheim on Morality and Society*, ed. Robert N. Bellah (Chicago, IL: University of Chicago Press, 1973), 64.

75 *Emile Durkheim on Morality and Society*, 65.

76 *The Nuer* (Oxford: Clarendon Press, 1969). Cf. also P. Coatalen's account, "La Notion de Segmentarité," in *Annales marocaines de sociologie* (Rabat: l'Institut de Sociologie de Rabat, 1968).

77 *Emile Durkheim on Morality and Society*, 67.

78 Jeanne Favret, "Relations de dépendance et manipulation de la violence en Kabylie," *L'Homme* (October–December, 1968), 24–25. This excellent article forms the basis of our reflections on the segmentary system in Arab societies. T.N. Translation is mine.

79 Emile Durkheim, *The Division of Labor in Society*, trans. W. D. Halls (New York: Simon & Schuster, 1997), 129. Durkheim explicitly refers to the book by V. Hanoteau and Letourneux, *La Kabylie et les coutumes kabyles*, 3 vols. (Paris: Imprimerie Impériale, 1872–1873). Cf. for a critique of this book, see the above-mentioned article by J. Favret.

80 Favret, "Relations de dépendance et manipulation de la violence en Kabylie."

81 Ernest Gellner, *Saints of the Atlas* (London: Weidenfeld and Nicolson, 1969).

82 Jacques Berque, *Structures sociales du Haut Atlas* (Paris: PUF, 1955). Cf. by the same author "Cent vingt ans de sociologie maghrébine," *Annales E.S.C.* (Paris: July–September, 1956).

83 Cf. P. Coatalen, "La Notion de Segmentarité," 189.
84 From whom we borrow several suggestions. T.N. Unpublished work; translations are mine.
85 And also those of J. Berque, G. Lazarev, A. Laroui, and A. Lahlimi.
86 Loc. cit., unpublished.
87 Ibid.
88 We refer the reader to his two articles: "Clan, lignage et communauté locale dans une tribu rifaine," *Revue de géographie du Maroc*, no. 8, Rabat, 1965, 25–33, and "Segmentary systems and the role of 'five fifths' in tribal Morocco," *Revue de l'Occident musulman et de la Méditerranée*, Summer 1967, Aix-en-Provence ["Segmentary Systems and the Role of 'Five Fifths' in Tribal Morocco," in Akbar S. Ahmed and David M. Hart (eds.), *Islam in Tribal Societies: From the Atlas to the Indus* (London: Routledge and Kegan Paul, 1984), 66–105].
89 Whose interesting book is little known: *Tribes of the Rif*, Harvard African Studies (Cambridge, MA: Peabody Museum of Harvard University, 1931).
90 This organization is noted to exist in the Draa by A. Hammoudi, whose research is ongoing.
91 Cf. C. Lévi-Strauss, *Finale, L'Homme nu, Mythologiques IV* (Paris: Plon, 1971) [*The Naked Man, Mythologiques Vol. 4*, trans. John Weightman and Doreen Weightman (Chicago, IL: University of Chicago Press, 1981)].
92 Cf. V. Propp, *Morphologie du conte* (Paris: Le Seuil, 1970) [(*Morphology of the Folktale*, trans. Laurence Scott (Austin: University of Texas Press, 1968)].
93 J. Waterbury, *The Commander of the Faithful: The Moroccan Political Elite, A Study in Segmented Politics* (New York: Columbia University Press, 1970).

3 Disoriented Orientalism

On the book by Jacques Berque, *Langages arabes du présent* (Paris: Gallimard, 1974) [*Cultural Expression in Arab Society Today*, trans. Robert W. Stookey (Austin: University of Texas Press, 1978)].

1 T.N. All translations from this book are mine. T.N. *Such a Deathly Desire*, trans. Russell Ford (Albany: State University of New York Press, 2007).

2 Berque, *Langages arabes du présent*.

3 Ibid., 339.

4 Cf. Michaux-Bellaire, *La Mission scientifique du Maroc* (Rabat: Service des Renseignements, 1925). T.N. Translation is mine.

5 Cf. Henry Corbin's introduction to his translation of Mulla Sadra, *Le Livre des pénétrations métaphysiques* (Tehran: Département d'Iranologie de l'Institut Franco-Iranien/Paris: Adrien-Maisonneuve, 1964).

6 Berque, *Langages arabes du présent*, 349.

7 Ibid., 350.

8 Jacques Berque and Louis Massignon, "Dialogue Sur 'Les Arabes,'" *Esprit* (1940–), no. 288 (10), 1960, 1505–1519. *JSTOR*, www.jstor.org/stable/24260594. T.N. Translations from this text are mine.

9 Ibid.

10 Christian personalism, however, has had two heirs in the Arab world: René Habachi and Mohammed Aziz Lahbabi.

11 Ibid.

12 Ibid.

13 Ibid.

14 Berque, *Langages arabes du présent*, 14.

15 Ibid., 242.

16 Jacques Berque, "Perspectives de l'orientalisme contemporaine," *Revue de l'Institut de belles lettres arabes* 20 (1957), 238. Berque's inaugural lecture at the Collège de France.

17 Gilles Deleuze, *Logique du sens*, coll. 10/18 (1973), 357 [*The Logic of Sense*, trans. Constantin V. Boundas (London: Continuum, 2004), 299].

18 Cf. Maxime Rodinson, "The Western Image and Western Studies of Islam," in *The Legacy of Islam*, ed. Joseph Schacht and C. E. Bosworth (Oxford: Clarendon Press, 1974).

19 Berque, *Langages arabes du présent*, 283.

20 *Jemaa*: traditional rural community.

21 Jacques Berque, *Dépossession du monde* (Paris: Le Seuil, 1964). T.N. Translations from this book are mine.

22 *Bulletin d'information du Maroc*, October 1945. T.N. Translation is mine.

23 Berque, *Langages arabes du présent*, 57.

24 Ibid., 241.
25 Ibid., 355.
26 Ibid., 10.
27 Ibid., 7.
28 Ibid., 63.
29 Ibid., 36.
30 Ibid., 355.
31 T.N. Translation is mine.
32 Cf. Goethe's notes, *Divan occidental-oriental*, trans. H. Lichtenberger
    (Paris: Aubier, 1940). T.N. Translations are mine.
33 Ibid., 67.
34 Ibid., 186.
35 T.N. *L'Occident comme l'Orient / T'offrent à goûter des choses pures. / Laisse là
    les caprices, laisse l'écorce, / Assieds-toi au grand festin: / Tu ne voudrais pas,
    même en passant, / Dédaigner ce plat.* Unable to find the English translation
    of this first part of the poem, I have translated it from the French, trying to
    match the tone with M. Bidney's translation of the second part.
36 T.N. *West-East Divan*, Johann Wolfgang von Goethe, trans. Martin
    Bidney, http://www.katharinamommsen.org/pdf/Divan/Divan-English-
    complete.pdf.

4 Sexuality according to the Quran

1 This study is a specific and indirect response to the book by Abdelwahab
   Bouhdiba, *La Sexualité en Islam* (Paris: PUF, 1975) [*Sexuality in Islam*,
   trans. Alan Sheridan (London: Routledge, 2008)]. The author uses both
   theology and sacred texts against sociology and vice versa, in such a
   way that in the final analysis the book remains enclosed in "patriarchal"
   ideology.
2 T.N. The word is *haya* in Arabic.
3 Cf. the chapter entitled "Rhetoric of the Coitus" of my book *La Blessure
   du nom propre* (Paris: Denoël, 1974), as well as my essay *De la mille et
   troisième nuit* (Tangier: Éditions marocaines et internationales, 1980),
   which deals with the relationship between the narrative on the one hand
   and patriarchy and death on the other.

4 *Volonté de savoir* (Paris: Gallimard, 1976), 76. T.N. Translation is taken
   from *The History of Sexuality, Volume 1: An Introduction*, trans. Robert
   Hurley (New York: Vintage, 1990), 57.

5 Which is not to say that pre-Islam has nothing to say on sexuality. The
   poetry of this epoch is by itself a major archaic testimony on sexuality
   and love among the Arabs.

6 Tahar Labib, *La Poésie amoureuse des Arabes* (Algiers: SNED, 1974). Let
   us note that in his above-mentioned book, Bouhdiba makes use of several
   themes from Labib's book (otherwise pertinent) without ever mentioning
   the author.

7 T.N. Sigmund Freud, "Resistances to Psychoanalysis," in *The Standard
   Edition of the Complete Psychological Works of Sigmund Freud, Vol. 19*,
   trans. James Strachey (London: Hogarth Press, 1925), 218.

8 Labib, *La Poésie amoureuse des Arabes*, 15. T.N. Translation is mine.

9 Cf. the first chapter of his bio-bibliography of Arab scholars and
   writers: *Mu'jam al-udabā*. T.N. Translation is mine.

10 We are using here the translation by Blachère, but with modifications
   on certain—essential—points (Paris: Éd. Maisonneuve et Larose, 1966).
   Our analysis rests first and foremost on the Arabic text of the Quran,
   and the translation intervenes in our study already as an interpretation.
   T.N. Translations of the Quran from the French are mine, which I have
   carried out based on the French text and through a comparison of
   various translations of the Surahs into English. I have also included
   Abdullah Yusuf Ali's translation of the Surahs in question, for comparison
   [Abdullah Yusuf Ali, *The Holy Quran* (Ware: Wordsworth Editions,
   2001)]. The Surah titles are also based on the Yusuf Ali version. The Yusuf
   Ali translation of these verses is as follows: "They are your garments and
   ye are their garments. (. . .); so now associate with them, and seek what
   Allah Hath ordained for you, (. . .)"

11 T.N. My translation of the terms *langage* and *langue* are based on the
   book *Saussure: Signs, System and Arbitrariness*, by David Holdcroft
   (New York: Cambridge University Press, 1991).

12 We refer the reader to the important work by Mohammed Arkoun, and
   in particular his introduction to the Quran, translated into the French by
   Kasimirski (*Le Coran*, Paris: Garnier-Flammarion, 1970). Based
   on his reading protocol of the Quran, he identifies three moments:

"1) a linguistic moment, which will allow us to discover a deeper order beneath the apparent disorder; 2) an anthropological moment, which will consist in recognizing the language of mythical structure in the Quran; and 3) a historical content in which the scope and limitations of logico-lexicographic exegeses and imaginative exegeses that Muslims have attempted to this day will be defined" (p. 15). T.N. Translation is mine. Cf. likewise, his "Introduction à la pensée Islamique classique" ("Introduction to classical Islamic thought"), in *Essais sur la pensée Islamique* (Paris: Éd. Maisonneuve et Larose, 1973). Other works in this direction are yet to be published. We look forward to them.

13 *The Holy Quran*: "He is Allah, the One and Only; Allah the eternal, Absolute; He begetteth not, nor is He begotten; And there is none like unto Him."

14 *The Holy Quran*: "And He taught Adam the nature of all things."

15 *The Holy Quran*: "And He taught Adam the nature of all things; then He placed them before the angels, and said: 'Tell me the nature of these if ye are right.'"

"They said: 'Glory to Thee, of knowledge We have none, save what Thou Hast taught us: In truth it is Thou Who art perfect in knowledge and wisdom.'"

16 T.N. I have translated *jouissance* by different terms when necessary, retaining the original French word in square brackets every time.

17 T.N. In various translations of the verse in question, this word is translated both in the sense of "provision" and "enjoyment"— corresponding to two meanings of *jouissance*. I have retained the sense of "provision" in this case and have translated it as "enjoyment" in a recurrence of the same verse further below.

18 *The Holy Quran*: "He said: 'O Adam! Tell them their natures.' When he had told them, Allah said: 'Did I not tell you that I know the secrets of heaven and earth, and I know what ye reveal and what you conceal?'"

"And behold, We said to the angels: 'Bow down to Adam' and they bowed down. Not so Iblis: he refused and he was haughty: he was of those who reject Faith."

"We said: 'O Adam! dwell thou and thy wife in the Garden; and eat of the bountiful things therein as (where and when) ye will; but approach not this tree, or ye run into harm and transgression.'"

"Then did Satan make them slip from the (garden), and get them out of the state (of felicity) in which they had been. We said: 'Get ye down, all (ye people), with enmity between yourselves. On earth will be your dwelling-place and your means of livelihood—for a time.'"

19 *The Holy Quran*: "O Adam! Dwell thou and thy wife in the Garden, and enjoy (its good Things) as ye wish: but approach not this tree, or ye run into harm and transgression."

"Then began Satan to whisper suggestions to them, bringing openly before their minds all their shame that was hidden from them (before): he said: 'Your Lord only forbade you this tree, lest ye should become angels or such beings as live for ever.'"

"And he swore to them both, that he was their sincere adviser."

"So by deceit he brought about their fall: when they tasted of the tree, their shame became manifest to them, and they began to sew together the leaves of the garden over their bodies. And their Lord called unto them: 'Did I not forbid you that tree, and tell you that Satan was an avowed enemy unto you?'"

"They said: 'Our Lord! We have wronged our own souls: If thou forgive us not and bestow not upon us Thy Mercy, we shall certainly be lost.'"

"((Allah)) said: 'Get ye down. With enmity between yourselves. On earth will be your dwelling-place and your means of livelihood—for a time.'"

"He said: 'Therein shall ye live, and therein shall ye die; but from it shall ye be taken out (at last).'"

"O ye Children of Adam! We have bestowed raiment upon you to cover your shame, as well as to be an adornment to you. But the raiment of righteousness—that is the best. Such are among the Signs of Allah, that they may receive admonition!"

"O ye Children of Adam! Let not Satan seduce you, in the same manner as He got your parents out of the Garden (…)"

20 Cf. the chapter: "Oedipus complex or Abraham complex?" in our book entitled *Vomito blanco* (*le sionisme et la conscience malheureuse*) [*Zionism and the unhappy consciousness*] (Paris: 10/18, 1974).

21 Cf. Kierkegaard's *Fear and Trembling* and the Abrahamic figure in *Glas* by Jacques Derrida (Paris: Galilée, 1974/re-edition Paris: Ed.

Denoël-Gonthier, 1981) [*Glas*, trans. John P. Leavey, Jr. and Richard Rand (Lincoln and London: University of Nebraska Press, 1986)]. It is needless to say that *Glas* is an exceptional text, but it is often forgotten.

22 *The Holy Quran*: "Ladies said in the City: 'The wife of the (great) Aziz is seeking to seduce her slave from his (true) self: Truly hath he inspired her with violent love: we see she is evidently going astray.'"

"When she heard of their malicious talk, she sent for them and prepared a banquet for them: she gave each of them a knife: and she said (to Joseph), 'Come out before them.' When they saw him, they did not extol him, and (in their amazement) cut their hands: they said, '(Allah) preserve us! No mortal is this! This is none other than a noble angel!'"

23 *The Holy Quran*: "It was just like this (. . .)"

24 *The Holy Quran*: "She was asked to enter the lofty Palace: but when she saw it, she thought it was a lake of water, and she (tucked up her skirts), uncovering her legs. He said: 'This is but a palace paved smooth with slabs of glass.'"

25 *The Holy Quran*: "Muhammad is not the father of any of your men, but (he is) the Messenger of Allah, and the Seal of the Prophets (. . .)"

26 *The Holy Quran*: "The Prophet is closer to the Believers than their own selves, and his wives are their mothers. Blood-relations among each other have closer personal ties, in the Decree of Allah. Than (the Brotherhood of) Believers and Muhajirs (. . .)"

27 *The Holy Quran*: "nevertheless do ye what is just to your closest friends: such is the writing in the Decree (of Allah)."

28 *The Holy Quran*: "Ye are not like any of the (other) women (. . .)"

29 *The Holy Quran*: "And Allah only wishes to remove all abomination from you, ye members of the Family, and to make you pure and spotless."

30 *The Holy Quran*: "this is a most serious slander!"

5 Bilingualism and Literature

1 Cf. letter-preface to Marc Gontard's book *Violence du texte* (Paris: L'Harmattan; Rabat: SMER, 1981).

2 Abdelwahab Meddeb, *Talismano* (Paris: Éd. Christian Bourgois, 1979). T.N. All translations from the novel are from *Talismano*, trans. Jane Kuntz

(Champaign and London: Dalkey Archive Press, 2011). Throughout the text, I have included the page numbers to the English translation in parentheses.

3 T.N. Depending on the context, it can mean "to," "at," "in," "on," "with," as well as necessitate other renderings.

4 T.N. *jouissance*.

5 T.N. Kateb Yacine, *Le Polygone étoilé* (Paris: Éditions du Seuil, 1966). Cited in Abdelkebir Khatibi, "Diglossia," trans. Whitney Sanford, in *Algeria in Other's Languages*, ed. Anne-Emmanuelle Berger (Ithaca and London: Cornell University Press, 2002).

6 T.N. *s'affoler*—according to the Littré, *affolement* is the act of becoming mad, especially with love.

7 T.N. "I am moving toward the calligraphers now. On the tight weft of the red fabric, they have written these words from Hallāj, purged of their theocentrism: *The point is the principle of any line, and the line is but an assemblage of points. And all lines, straight or curved, spring from this same point. And anything that falls under our gaze is a point between two others. Here is evidence that* [the void] *is apparent through each act of contemplation. This is why I declare, there is nothing in which I do not see nothingness* [the void]! (113).

6 Questions of Art

1 T.N. Paul Klee, *Paul Klee* (New York: Parkstone Press International, 2013), 170.

2 T.N. Ibid., 182.

3 T.N. Ibid., 150.

4 T.N. Paul Klee, "Trip to Tunisia," in *The Diaries of Paul Klee: 1898–1918*, ed. Felix Klee, trans. Pierre B. Schneider, R. Y. Zachary, and Max Knight (Berkeley: University of California Press, 1968), 220, 297.

5 T.N. All translations from Delacroix's letters are mine.

6 Eugène Delacroix, *Journal de Eugène Delacroix* (Paris: Plon, 1893).

7 I presented part of this lecture, on the subject of *Art in Islam*, before different audiences.

8   See our book in collaboration with Mohammed Sijelmassi, *L'art
    calligraphique arabe* (Paris: Chêne, 1976; Gallimard, 1994) [*The Splendor
    of Islamic Calligraphy*, trans. James Huges (London: Thames & Hudson,
    1996)].

9   See the remarkable work by A. Papadopoulo, *L'Islam et l'Art musulman*
    (Paris: Mazenod, 1976) [*Islam and Muslim Art*, trans. Robert Erich Wolf
    (New York: Harry N. Abrams, 1994)]. I owe a number of comments
    to him.

10 Taine, *Philosophie de l'art*, vol. 1 (Paris: Slatkine, 1980), 82. T.N.
    Translation is mine. Khatibi seems to be mistaken as to the author of
    these words.

11 T.N. Translation is mine.

12 *La Dissymétrie* (Paris: Gallimard, 1973), 18. T.N. Translation is mine.

13 T.N. Citation taken from "Dynamics of Dissymmetry," trans. Mary
    Fradier, *Diogenes* 19 (76): 62–92 (Winter 1971), an earlier version of *La
    Dissymétrie*, published in English. "Rose-window" designates here what
    I have rendered as *rosace*.

14 Caillois, *La Dissymétrie*, 75. T.N. Translation is mine.

15 T.N. *Glas*, trans., John P. Leavey, Jr. and Richard Rand (Lincoln and
    London: University of Nebraska Press, 1986), 22.

16 T.N. Translation is mine.

17 Papadopoulo, *L'Islam et l'Art musulman*, 238. T.N. Translation is mine.

18 T.N. Translation is mine. *The Holy Quran*: "Glory to (Allah) Who did take
    His servant for a Journey by night from the Sacred Mosque to the farthest
    Mosque, whose precincts We did bless–in order that We might show him
    some of Our signs: for He is the One Who heareth and seeth (all things)."
    Abdullah Yusuf Ali (Ware: Wordsworth, 2001).

19 T.N. Translation is mine.

Index

origin 26, 30, 81, 86, 97, 122, 129,
    136, 138, 149–50, 157 (*see also*
    originarity)
originarity *see asala*
other 3, 11, 16, 19, 73, 85, 89, 104,
    131, 134, 136 (*see also* alterity;
    difference)
other-thought 1–3, 5–6, 9, 19, 21,
    25, 27–8, 30, 35, 38, 98, 162,
    172 (*see also* plural thought;
    unthought)
outside 16, 23, 27, 31, 33, 38, 41, 91,
    122, 125

palimpsest 99, 104, 106, 133–4,
    137–9, 156
Papadopoulo, Alexandre 167
Pascon, Paul 67–8
philosophy 6, 19, 36 (*see also*
    metaphysics)
    Arab 9, 10, 14
    of Enlightenment 78
    in Islam 13
Plato 97, 150
plural thought 4, 6, 21, 30
plurilingualism 117, 119, 125–6, 134
    (*see also* bilingualism)
poetry 21, 124
    Berque and 86, 87, 90–2
precolonial hierarchy 38–53, 60
prophecy 18, 31, 42, 113
psychoanalysis 14, 83, 97, 127–8

Quran 9, 78, 95–116, 122, 132,
    135–6, 151, 154–5, 162

rationalism 12, 17, 77–8
representation 7, 18, 146–7, 151, 161,
    173
rosace 152–3, 158–62

Salafism 11–12, 16–17
science 12, 14, 20, 26, 32–4, 36, 77,
    128, 145 (*see also* Salafism;
    technology)

Khaldunian 39–42
scienta sexualis 95
social 26, 28, 30, 32, 34, 36, 77, 80,
    82, 84
segmental (*see* segmentary system)
segmentary system 38, 53, 59–71
self-sufficiency 6, 26–8, 34 (*see also*
    ethnocentrism; imperialism)
simulacrum 9, 20, 22, 34, 76–77, 79,
    81–2, 84, 85, 87, 91, 107, 110,
    112, 128–9, 155–6, 160, 165, 173
sociology 12, 57, 70, 83–5
    decolonization of 25–38
Solomon 109–10
speak in tongues 35, 38, 123, 126,
    131–2, 138
speech 26, 28, 32–3, 36–7, 163
    dialectical 127
    ethnocentric 34
    maternal 124, 127–8, 133 (*see also*
        mother tongue)
State 43, 46, 48–9, 51, 53, 56, 58–9, 68
    (*see also* Makhzen)
symmetry
    art 152, 156–61

Talismano 117–40
technology 6, 12, 16, 20–2, 26, 77, 79–
    80, 88–9, 93, 145, 150 (*see also*
    metaphysics; Salafism; science)
text 10–11, 90–1, 117–20, 122, 124–8,
    130–2, 137–9, 151, 164 (*see also*
    language; translation; writing)
theology 2, 8–10, 12–16, 19, 22–3, 35,
    76, 87, 98, 136, 145, 155, 161,
    165–7
    Abrahamic theology 81, 164
Third World 4, 6, 25–6, 28, 30, 36, 75
tradition 7–8, 11–12, 15–17, 33, 40
traditionalism (*see* tradition)
transgression 2, 6–7, 103, 107–8, 164
translation 9, 10, 18, 31, 35,
    89–90, 95, 99, 117–40 (*see
    also* bilingualism; language;
    plurilingualism; untranslatable)